ARTICLES of FAITH

ARTICLES of FAITH

What Nazarenes Believe and Why

Compiled by
GAY LEONARD

Beacon Hill Press of Kansas City
Kansas City, Missouri

Copyright 2005
by Beacon Hill Press of Kansas City

ISBN 083-412-2154

Printed in the
United States of America

Cover Design: Paul Franitza

Library of Congress Cataloging-in-Publication Data

Parrott, Leslie, 1922-
   Who is the Holy Spirit?/ by Leslie Parrott.
      p. cm.
   ISBN 0-8341-2210-3 (pbk.)
   1. Holy Spirit. I. Title.

   BT121.3.P37 2005
   231'.3—dc22

                                                    2005002635

10 9 8 7 6 5 4

Contents

Foreword

Articles of Faith. For Nazarenes, those words embody a core sense of the identity of our denomination. They are the most succinct expression of the beliefs that form the life of the church. Carefully crafted by the general assemblies of the Church of the Nazarene over the history of our existence, these articles provide the essential "glue" that binds the church into a unified and cohesive whole.

These articles are not merely abstract ideas. They are the soul of the Church of the Nazarene. We have no reason to exist as a global body apart from the unifying expression of our beliefs as they are articulated in these articles.

And these are not the mere ideas of men and women who gather periodically to craft a consensus in order to maintain a human institution. We believe these to be the succinct description of the teachings of the Word of God, the Holy Bible. We believe they are the basis on which this church, a particular expression of the larger Body of Christ, may find its reason to exist.

These articles are not theoretical. They are intensely practical. They describe beliefs that define practices. We live by these articles. They help us to understand our relationship with God, with one another, and with the world around us.

This study of the *Articles of Faith* of the Church of the Nazarene provides the church with a fresh and contemporary explanation of these vital statements. Like the articles themselves, this study is intentionally brief. It is not intended to provide comprehensive justification or defense of the articles. That is the purview of theologians, scholars, pastors, and denominational leaders. This is for understanding. This is a "church book," intended to help us all have a clearer understanding of what these articles teach us, how they find expression in our homes, our schools, and our churches. The study materials at the end of each chapter will help us transform these statements of belief into daily living.

The Church of the Nazarene is a message-driven institution. The message that brought this church into being is founded on the redemptive purposes of a loving God who sent His Son into the world to reconcile the world to himself. He has desired that we know Him, that we be like Him. He has made it clear that we can love others as He has loved us. He has made this possible through the sufferings of Christ on our behalf and through the effective working of the Holy Spirit in our lives. This message is desperately important to us and to the world to which we are called to minister. It is therefore essential that we not only believe these things but also that these things we believe actually determine how we will live and relate to one another and to the world around us.

Without this message, we have no mission. And without a mission, we have no message. The two are inextricably intertwined. Either these beliefs shape us and our life together, or they have no meaning at all. Either they drive us to a broken world with passion and holy love, or our beliefs are sterile and ineffective.

So this is life. This is who we are. And this is how we live. Read it. Linger long over it, and let it shape not only what you believe but also how you live.

—*Jesse C. Middendorf*
General Superintendent
Church of the Nazarene

Acknowledgments

Special appreciation is expressed to Rob Staples, Stan Ingersol, Hans Zimmerman, Carolyn Hampton, Sherry Pinson, Brent Cobb, Fred Huff, and Roderick Leupp.

Preamble

In order that we may preserve our God-given heritage, the faith once delivered to the saints, especially the doctrine and experience of entire sanctification as a second work of grace, and also that we may cooperate effectually with other branches of the Church of Jesus Christ in advancing God's kingdom, we, the ministers and lay members of the Church of the Nazarene, in accordance with the principles of constitutional legislation established among us, do hereby ordain, adopt, and set forth as the fundamental law or Constitution of the Church of the Nazarene the *Articles of Faith.*

                              —*Manual*, Church of the Nazarene

1
THE TRIUNE GOD

We believe in one eternally existent, infinite God, Sovereign of the universe; that He only is God, creative and administrative, holy in nature, attributes, and purpose; that He, as God, is Triune in essential being, revealed as Father, Son, and Holy Spirit.

—*Manual*, Article 1

Every Christian act and impulse—praying, witnessing, believing, singing, worshiping—arises and is nurtured by the Christian confession of who God is and how He moves the world through love. The Christian God is God the Father, God the Son, and God the Holy Spirit, the thrice-blessed name of the holy Trinity. The Church's great hymn writers have instinctually known that this is the God who must be praised.

> *Holy, holy, holy! Lord God Almighty! . . .*
> *God in three Persons, blessed Trinity!*
> —Reginald Heber

> *Come, Thou Almighty King . . .*
> *Come, Thou Incarnate Word . . .*
> *Come, Holy Comforter . . .*
> *To Thee, great One in Three.*
> —Anonymous

The Church prays to the Father, through the mediating ministry of the Son, in the empowering enablement of God the Spirit. Early artistic renderings of the Trinity often represented this truth. The crucified Christ is seen reclining in the

Father's bosom, for only through the blood of the Son are we reconciled to God. In the midst of Father and Son, the Holy Spirit hovers as a dove, for He is the richly and freely endowed "bond of love" between Father and Son.

The doctrine of the Trinity may be the one Christian teaching that moves from 0 to 60 in six seconds, from relative clarity to befuddlement in no time flat. Although the word "Trinity" does not appear in the New Testament and was not known until the *Latin Trinitas*, coined by the Church father Tertullian (c. 160-220), all Christians know the word and most can give a rudimentary explanation of the Three-in-One and the One-in-Three. After that, however, most people —even many pastors—are lost. Practically speaking, Christians overwhelmingly are mere monotheists rather than fully realized Trinitarians.

Not everyone can have the Sistine Chapel in the backyard for private meditation. But imagine a place within your reach where beauty is beyond description and truth beyond question. Would you not spend as much of your life there as possible?

The simple beauty of God as triune is that this is who God reveals himself to be. God has brought the Sistine Chapel to your backyard. Why not experience God as He wills himself to be known, loved, and worshiped by those He created for this express purpose? The doctrine of the Trinity is the strongest possible theological, spiritual, and even ethical statement God can make to us. It is not human ingenuity and curiosity that have erected some unknown and unknowable doctrine, although too frequently this has happened. The Trinity is the gospel of God, the only divine offer to take human life into divine life and transform it. As great Trinitarian theologian Karl Barth put it, the Trinity means that God perfectly corresponds to himself. Of none other can this be said.

Historically, the headwaters of the doctrine of the Trinity are found in Jesus' bold assertion of His oneness with the Father (John 10:30), a claim that led directly to His death. When at Christmas we sing "Word of the Father, now in flesh appearing!" (John F. Wade, "O Come, All Ye Faithful"), we acknowledge that the Father's eternal Word, coming into flesh in Jesus Christ, is in reality "very God of very God . . . being of one substance with the Father" (Nicene Creed).

The Holy Spirit is by no means an afterthought. This Spirit is, with the Son, coequal and coeternal with the Father. He may be the Third Person of the Trinity, but He is God's first response and first overture of peace and healing to this cruel world. The Holy Spirit appears in the Bible's first paragraph as the Presence of God brooding over the waters (Gen. 1:2).

Is there a distinctive Nazarene approach to the Trinity? Not if it will remove Nazarenes from the great ecumenical consensus that from the beginning of Christian history has confessed God as Father, Son, and Spirit. Yet the Nazarene emphasis on the love and grace of God and on seeking full conformity to the heart of Jesus Christ is a perfect fit with God's triune nature.

The heart of Jesus Christ is to do His Father's will in the constant embrace of the Spirit's anointing. The Triune God is, as someone has so well expressed it, "no solitary God." He is rather a Community-in-Love, where each of the three Persons pours His life out for the other two and receives His life back from Them. Our best human analogy, any family that constantly practices other-regarding love, is only a flickering wick next to the Trinity's brilliance.

C. S. Lewis said it best: "We [as Christians] trust, not because 'a God' exists, but because this God exists" ("On Obstinacy in Belief," from *The World's Last Night and Other Essays*). John Wesley closed his sermon "The New Creation" with a beautiful testimony centering God's power to make all things new exactly in His very being as triune: "And, to crown all, there will be a deep, an intimate, an uninterrupted union with God; a constant communion with the Father and his Son Jesus Christ, through the Spirit; a continual enjoyment of the Three-One God, and of all the creatures in him!"

Roderick T. Leupp lives in Bartlesville, Oklahoma, with his wife, Stephanie, and their children, Emily and Rebecca.

Quote Rack

You, O eternal Trinity, are a deep sea, into which the more I enter the more I find, and the more I find the more I seek. The soul cannot be satiated in your abyss, for she continually hungers after you, the eternal Trinity, desiring to see you with the light of your light.   —Catherine of Siena

The doctrine of the blessed Trinity is a reminder of the supernaturalness of biblical Christianity. The doctrine defies rationalization, yet it provides for the believer the answer to the unity and diversity of the world.   —Robert P. Lightner

Footprints

The Early Church was troubled by heresy even before the writing of the New Testament was concluded. One heresy concerning the Trinity was promoted by Origen, an influential teacher of the third century. Origen taught subordination of the Divine Persons: God as preeminent over the Son and the Holy Spirit, and the Three Persons as coeternal but not coequal. He instructed believers to pray only to God the Father, believing that prayers directed to the Son and the Holy Spirit were sinful.

We recognize that because God is triune, prayer must be voiced to the Triune God with no hint of subordination. The Father is the "goal" of prayer, Jesus Christ the "road or bridge," and the Holy Spirit the "motive power" driving the believer along the way of the Son toward the Father (C. S. Lewis, *Mere Christianity*). To pray to God is to engage the Trinity.

Ponder and Pursue

The names of God have specific meanings and therefore are like a picture of Him or a promise from Him. Examine these scriptures to study a few of the names of God.

EL SHADDAI: "God Almighty" is used 48 times in the Old Testament, 31 times in Job alone (Gen. 17:1).

JEHOVAH-JIREH: "The Lord Will Provide" comes from the Hebrew for "to see" or "to foresee." He recognizes our needs and provides (Gen. 22:14).

JEHOVAH-M'KADDESH: "The Lord Who Sanctifies" makes whole or sets apart for holiness (Exod. 31:13; Lev. 20:8).

JEHOVAH-SHALOM: "The Lord Our Peace" brings peace derived from being a "whole" person in right relationship to God and to one's fellow human being (Judg. 6:24).

JEHOVAH-TSIDKENU: "The Lord Our Righteousness" comes from *tsidek*, straight, balanced as on scales, thereby the full weight, right, righteous (Jer. 23:5-6; 33:16).

JEHOVAH-ROHI: "The Lord Our Shepherd" derives from *ro'eh*, to pasture (Ps. 23:1).

JEHOVAH-SHAMMAH: "The Lord Is There," ever-present (Ezek. 48:35).

Some of the most prominent names of God are plural, suggesting the three-in-one nature of the Trinity.

EL, God, "mighty, strong, prominent," is used approximately 250 times in the Old Testament (Gen. 1:1). *ELOHIM*, the plural form of *EL*, is used with singular verbs.

JEHOVAH, "Lord" (translated in all capitals). *YAHWEH* is the covenant name of God, occurring more than 6,800 times in the Old Testament (Exod. 6:3). From the verb "to be," *YAHWEH* is "The Self-Existent One," "I AM WHO I AM," or "I WILL BE WHO I WILL BE," as revealed to Moses at the burning bush (Exod. 3). Deut. 6:4-5 uses both *JEHOVAH* and *ELOHIM* to indicate one God with a plurality of persons.

ADONAI: "Lord" (only the "L" capitalized) is used 300 times in the Old Testament, always plural when referring to God. Whenever singular, the reference is to a human lord or master. (Note both Jehovah "Lord" and Adonai "Lord" in Ps. 110:1.)

Additional Scripture References

Gen. 1; Lev. 19:2; Deut. 6:4-5; Isa. 5:16; 6:1-7; 40:18-31; Matt. 3:16-17; 28:19-20; John 14:6-27; 1 Cor. 8:6; 2 Cor. 13:14; Gal. 4:4-6; Eph. 2:13-18.

2
JESUS CHRIST

We believe in Jesus Christ, the Second Person of the Triune Godhead; that He was eternally one with the Father; that He became incarnate by the Holy Spirit and was born of the Virgin Mary, so that two whole and perfect natures, that is to say the Godhead and manhood, are thus united in one Person very God and very man, the God-man.

We believe that Jesus Christ died for our sins, and that He truly arose from the dead and took again His body, together with all things appertaining to the perfection of man's nature, wherewith He ascended into heaven and is there engaged in intercession for us.

—*Manual*, Article 2

Ask, "Who is Jesus?" and Christians will often respond, "The Son of God . . . and Mary's child." As simple as this response sounds, a rich and intriguing history lies behind it. The Christian confession of Jesus' identity did not arise overnight. Rather, it emerged as God's people attempted to make sense of His being both divine and human. Briefly stated, Christians believe that Jesus Christ is "very God and very man" (*Manual*, Article 2).

Although the New Testament refers to Jesus as both Son of God (divine) and Son of Man (human), it does not attempt to reconcile these references. As a result, early Christians tended to emphasize either Jesus' divinity over His humanity or His humanity over His divinity. These tendencies fueled many heresies, and early Christian councils tackled the question "How are we to understand Jesus Christ?"

Early Christians were often influenced by the popular belief that all material things, including the human body, were evil. Accepting the humanity of Jesus, some were reluctant to affirm that Jesus was actually divine. To avoid speaking of God in terms of flesh and blood, these Christians attempted to exalt Jesus without equating Him to God. Some spoke of Him as a member of the angelic host or as an emanation from God. Others insisted that as a creature, Jesus either was the first and highest of God's creation or was chosen as Messiah due to His perfect obedience to God's law. Others argued that the "divine Christ" had descended upon the "earthly Jesus," resulting in the coexistence of two persons.

Despite these explanations, the Church condemned as heresies all views that denied Christ's full and complete divinity. It affirmed that He forever has been divine and never ceased being divine during His lifetime. "He is the image of the invisible God" (Col. 1:15) and from the beginning is the Word that "was with God, and . . . was God" (John 1:1). Jesus entered into human history but was not created by it. In the words of the Nicene Creed, He was "begotten, not made." In affirming the divinity of Christ, the Church stressed that Jesus was "conceived by the Holy Spirit, born of the Virgin Mary" (Apostles' Creed).

Standing firm in its insistence that Jesus was "eternally one with the Father" (*Manual*, Article 2) while remaining resolute in the belief in one God, the Church grounded its understanding of Christ in the triune nature of God. Thus Christians confess Jesus to be the Second Person of the Trinity. As an appropriate understanding of Jesus emerges from God's triune nature, it is most fitting that the article of faith regarding Jesus Christ follows immediately after the one regarding the Triune God.

While some early Christians denied the divinity of Jesus, others denied His humanity. Again influenced by the belief that material things were evil, some who accepted the divinity of Christ concluded that He must not have been truly human; He only appeared to be human. Others reasoned that Jesus' human nature was absorbed into His divine nature so that during His lifetime He did not experience true humanity. However, just as the Church rejected all denials of Jesus' full divinity, it condemned all denials of His full humanity.

The Church instead affirmed the Incarnation, the belief that the divine Word became flesh and blood and lived a real human life. Rather than merely appearing as human, Jesus was fully and completely human. Our eyes saw Him; our ears heard Him; our hands touched Him (1 John 1:1). The Church confessed that He indeed "suffered . . . was crucified, dead, and buried" (Apostles' Creed). Because He developed in a naturally human way, faced temptation, knew physical suffering and grief, and experienced death, He genuinely sympathizes with our human experiences (Heb. 2:14-18). As the resurrected and ascended Lord, He is our empathizing priest who makes intercession on our behalf (Heb. 9:24; 10:19-20).

In the face of misunderstandings over Christ's identity, the Church confessed that two whole and perfect natures—divine and human—were united in the one Person, Jesus Christ. On the one hand, He was indeed "very God of very God"; on the other hand, He "was made man" (Nicene Creed). Centuries later, misunderstandings of Christ persist and are often naively accepted as valid. Some continue to speak of Jesus as if He were partially human and partially divine, while others speak of two distinct persons residing side-by-side within the one. Other popular misconceptions view Christ as being human at times and divine at other times or describe one nature as "taking over" or being "absorbed by" the other nature.

The Church continues to reject all such views and to confess that Jesus was fully divine and fully human throughout His life. In Jesus Christ we see God; in Jesus Christ we see humanity. In other words, in Christ, "two whole and perfect natures . . . Godhead and manhood, are thus united in one Person very God and very man, the God-man" (*Manual*, Article 2).

Tim Green is dean of the School of Religion at Trevecca Nazarene University, in Nashville.

Word Study

Messiah—from the Aramaic *məšiḥā*, meaning "the anointed one." It came to mean one anointed as savior or liberator. "Christ" in Greek is synonymous with the Hebrew "Messiah." "Christ" is a title, not a name. When we call Him "Jesus Christ," or more properly "Jesus the Christ," as Peter did in Luke 9:20, we are confessing our faith that He is the Messiah who was promised by the Old Testament prophets.

Quote Rack

He took upon Him the flesh in which we have sinned, that by wearing our flesh He might forgive sins; a flesh which He shares with us by wearing it, not by sinning in it. He blotted out through death the sentence of death that by a new creation of our race in himself He might sweep away the penalty appointed by the former Law. . . . For Scripture had foretold that He who is God should die; that the victory and triumph of them that trust in Him lay in the fact that He, who is immortal and cannot be overcome by death, was to die that mortals might gain eternity. —Hilary, *On the Trinity*

Ponder and Pursue

The names and titles of Jesus provide a rich and long Bible study. Here are only a few of them appearing in Scripture. Consider the meaning of each term and the qualities it ascribes to Jesus. Meditate on how each particular word picture enriches your understanding of His character.

Wonderful Counselor, Mighty God, Everlasting Father, Prince of Peace—Isa. 9:6
Jesus—Matt. 1:21
Immanuel—Matt. 1:23
The Holy One—Mark 1:24
The Christ—Mark 8:29
The Son of the Most High—Luke 1:32
The Word—John 1:1
The Lamb of God—John 1:29
Messiah—John 1:41

Savior—John 4:42
The Bread of Life—John 6:35
The Light of the World—John 8:12
The Gate—John 10:7
The Good Shepherd—John 10:11
The Way, the Truth, the Life—John 14:6
The Vine—John 15:5
High Priest—Heb. 7:26
Author and Perfecter of our faith—Heb. 12:2
The Living Stone—1 Pet. 2:4
The Capstone—1 Pet. 2:7
The Amen—Rev. 3:14
*The Alpha and the Omega, the First and the Last, the Beginning
    and the End*—Rev. 22:13
The Root and the Offspring of David—Rev. 22:16
The Bright Morning Star—Rev. 22:16

Additional Scripture References

Matt. 1:20-25; 16:15-16; Luke 1:26-35; John 1:1-18; Acts 2:22-36;
Rom. 8:3, 32-34; Gal. 4:4-5; Phil. 2:5-11; Col. 1:12-22; 1 Tim. 6:14-16;
Heb. 1:1-5; 7:22-28; 9:24-28; 1 John 1:1-3; 4:2-3, 15.

3
THE HOLY SPIRIT

We believe in the Holy Spirit, the Third Person of the Triune Godhead, that He is ever present and efficiently active in and with the Church of Christ, convincing the world of sin, regenerating those who repent and believe, sanctifying believers, and guiding into all truth as it is in Jesus.

—*Manual*, Article 3

The ancient Hebrews were nomadic. Even when they settled into towns and took on the appearance of stability, they remembered at the beginning of their creed, "My father was a wandering Aramean" (Deut. 26:5). Their word "spirit" is a word with movement all over it. It is "wind," "breath," "life." In Gen. 2, God scrapes together an Adam-sculpture from the dust of the earth and breathes into it, and it becomes a living hunger for more life, a hunger for the living God. The breath of God opens the density of compacted earth and fills what are now lungs, and Adam gets up and moves—by God's Spirit.

The word "holy" is a strong word to these people, one that speaks especially of the uniqueness of God. They also speak of other things as holy, such as a bowl or a knife used in worship, but those objects are not holy in themselves. They come to be holy as God makes use of them.

When these words are put together to form the phrase "Holy Spirit," they convey that a movement of life reaches out from the mystery of the Holy One and enters the world that is so different, bringing to it something of what God is and does. Since the Holy Spirit is the very life of God, not only does Adam get up, but also, in a different way, a prophet gets up who is inspired by the Spirit to proclaim the word of the Sovereign God.

The Holy Spirit in the gospel narratives moves into and about the words and work and very life of Jesus. The Spirit descends upon Him at His baptism, drives Him into the wilderness of temptation, is in His casting-out of demons, and most dramatically and importantly enters into His tomb, His death, and His damnation and saturates Him with holy life, thus raising Him from the dead.

God remains different but never aloof. God the Father sends the Son and the Spirit and calls a dying world into God's own mysterious, joyful, eternal life. And when Jesus is raised from the dead, God's Holy Spirit blows upon the world of the lost, gathering them together as a whirlwind might, making them a Church, drawing them into the very body of Jesus.

The Holy Spirit is God's life-giving entry into a world that otherwise would be dead and damned. To imagine this Spirit is to imagine those whom the Spirit has bathed with the mysterious way, truth, and life of the Holy One. To imagine the Spirit is to imagine the faces of the people who now live in the life of God's liberation, going where God has gone already in Jesus. To imagine the Spirit is to imagine the Church.

We say the Holy Spirit is a *person*, but this is not to say the Spirit is classified as one of us *people*. The Holy Spirit was called a person before it was common to call human beings persons. To say the Spirit is a person is simply to say He is different from God the Father and from God the Son, but the three of them dance together in such a way that they are one God. The perfect oneness of God occurs where Jesus touches real flesh-and-blood people. Of course, Jesus is a person as we are. Since there is no way to the mystery of God except through Jesus the human being, we must say the Spirit also is no abstract force but is as personal as Jesus is. God the Father also is personal in this sense.

The article of faith concerning the Holy Spirit has a long history behind it. The Holy Scriptures run through that history, but the history also includes what people embraced by the story of Jesus struggled to understand as they read and listened in their thanksgiving and worship. Speaking in detail of the Spirit as a "person," as one of "the Trinity," and cutting a certain path of salvation came slowly in the Church's story. However, if the article rings true, this is exactly what we would expect. The God of life is not frozen in a dense past. The truth that is Jesus is also a way and a life. We would expect, then, that as the people of God live on by God's grace, they might come to say something faithful both to what God has done and to what He is doing. It should not surprise us that the Church needed almost 400 years to come right out and say that the Holy Spirit is fully God. But it also should not surprise us that when it did so, it called the Holy Spirit "the Lord and Giver of life" (The Creed of Constantinople, A.D. 381).

Craig Keen is professor of systematic theology at Azusa Pacific University in Azusa, California.

Word Study

Holy—from the Indo-European root *kailo-*, meaning "whole, uninjured, of good omen." (Interestingly, this is the same root that produced the words "health" and "whole." See chapter 14: Divine Healing.) The Holy Spirit is one of the three persons of the Triune God in whom dwells the whole fullness of the divine nature. Likewise, humanity is not whole or complete in the image of God without the indwelling of the Holy Spirit.

Quote Rack

The temple itself is the heart of man, Christ is the high priest, who from thence sends up the incense of prayers, and joins them to His own intercession and presents all together to His Father; and the Holy Ghost by His dwelling there hath also consecrated it into a temple; and God dwells in our hearts by faith, and Christ by His Spirit, and the Spirit by His purities: so that we are also cabi-

nets of the mysterious Trinity, and what is this short of heaven itself, but as infancy is short of manhood?

—Jeremy Taylor, *Holy Living*

Footprints

The Church of the Nazarene was formed by the union of several
independent Holiness groups that formed between 1887 and 1904.
One of those was the Church of the Nazarene, an independent
church in Los Angeles under the leadership of Phineas F. Bresee.
Dr. Bresee became one of the principal founders of the present-day
denomination. In 1907 he was elected as the first general superintendent and served until 1915. Dr. Bresee maintained a strong emphasis that holiness and ministry to the poor must be primary reasons for the existence of the Church of the Nazarene. In 1901 he
wrote in the *Nazarene Messenger:* "The first miracle after the baptism of the Holy Ghost was wrought upon a beggar. It means that
the first service of a Holy Ghost-baptized church is to the poor; that
its ministry is to those who are lowest down; that its gifts are for
those who need them the most. As the Spirit was upon Jesus to
preach the gospel to the poor, so His Spirit is upon His servants for
the same purpose." (See Luke 4:17-21.)

Ponder and Pursue

Article 3 of the *Manual of the Church of the Nazarene* lists six
distinct aspects of the work and ministry of the Holy Spirit. For further understanding, read the accompanying scriptures.

The Third Person of the Triune Godhead (Gen. 1:2). How has the
Holy Spirit been at work since the beginning of creation?

*Ever present and efficiently active in and with the Church of
Christ* (Eph. 3:14-21). Because this was Paul's prayer for the church
at Ephesus, what does this say about the Spirit's activity within the
Church? How do these words encourage you personally as well?

Convincing the world of sin (John 16:7-11). What does it mean
to be convicted of your sins?

Regenerating those who repent and believe (Rom. 8:2). How are
we freed from the bondage of sin?

Sanctifying believers (Acts 15:8-9; 2 Thess. 2:13, 1 Pet. 1:2).
What is the relationship of purity of heart and the Holy Spirit?

Guiding into all truth as it is in Jesus (John 14:15-18, 26; 16:13).
How does the Holy Spirit teach us and guide us into all truth?

Additional Scripture References

John 7:39; 16:7-15; Acts 2:33; Rom. 8:1-27; Gal. 3:1-14; 4:6; 1 Thess. 4:7-8; 1 John 3:24; 4:13.

4

THE HOLY SCRIPTURES

We believe in the plenary inspiration of the Holy Scriptures, by which we understand the 66 books of the Old and New Testaments, given by divine inspiration, inerrantly revealing the will of God concerning us in all things necessary to our salvation, so that whatever is not contained therein is not to be enjoined as an article of faith.

—*Manual*, Article 4

The fourth Nazarene article of faith, "The Holy Scriptures," is part of our Protestant legacy. The historic ancient creeds of the Church, the Apostles', the Nicene, and the Athanasian say nothing about the nature of Scripture. But the basic issues of the Protestant Reformation included the content and role of Scripture and its authority for the Church. Changing approaches to the Bible with the rise of modernity brought specific attention to the inspiration of Scripture.

Our article affirms the "plenary inspiration of the Holy Scriptures." The word "plenary" means "full." By this affirmation Nazarenes declare their belief that Scripture is completely inspired by God—not just "sort of" inspired—and that all 66 books of the Old and New Testaments are inspired (*Manual*, Article 4). The word "plenary" also describes a middle ground in debates about inspiration. On one extreme are those, though few in recent years, who believe God dictated every word of Scripture to the biblical authors. On the other extreme are those who believe the Bible is the product of human authors inspired in the same sense that all great authors are inspired. "Plenary inspiration" acknowledges the important and influential role of the human authors but also affirms that this human process was the means by which God communicated the message He wanted to communicate.

The word "inspiration" comes from 2 Tim. 3:16, which describes all Scripture as inspired by God and "useful for teaching, rebuking, correcting and training." The *New International Version* translates the Greek very literally: "All Scripture is God-breathed." By describing Scripture as inspired or God-breathed, we affirm that God brings life, energy, renewal, and transformation through the Scriptures. The very life-giving breath of God is at work in the Bible.

One of the results of this inspiration is Scripture that "inerrantly reveal[s] the will of God concerning us in all things necessary to our salvation" (*Manual*, Article 4). Nazarenes affirm that Scripture contains no error at all when it comes to communicating to us everything we need to know to be saved. In the past 120 years, others have often used the word "inerrant" to describe a view of Scripture affirming no errors of any kind. For several reasons our article of faith does not make that claim.

First, we believe the subject and purpose of the Bible is to communicate to us the great message of the gospel, the word of salvation. The purpose is not to teach manners or culture or history or science. The purpose of Scripture is to bring us into right relationship with God and each other. This does not mean we necessarily think the Bible contains errors in history or science. Rather, we recognize that science and history represent the best human understanding available at any given time. Science and history develop and change as research continues. To spend energy showing how the Bible "fits" with science or history can easily distract us from the Bible's main purpose: to bring people into right relationship with God and each other.

Another reason Nazarenes have not devoted energy to defending the inerrancy of the Bible in all matters is that traditional defenders of that doctrine have affirmed only the inerrancy of the "autographs" of Scriptures, that is, the original writings before copies were made. No autographs are known to exist, and there is no prospect of finding any. It's better to focus on the purpose of the Scriptures we *do* have than to speculate about what must have been true in the autographs we do *not* have.

The beauty of our article on Scripture is that it emphasizes the most important aspects of the will of God to us. Sometimes we get caught up in wanting to know God's will for our lives in relatively minor issues. Some even suffer spiritual paralysis because they're not confident of God's will about eating this evening at home versus in a restaurant or vacationing in the mountains versus at the coast. The most important issue of our lives is whether we have come into saving relationship with God through Christ. We have no doubts or uncertainties about that primary matter. Scripture makes no error in communicating that to us!

Another way of saying this is that "whatever is not contained [in Scripture] is not to be enjoined as an article of faith" (*Manual*, Article 4). Scripture sufficiently contains everything we need to know about salvation. There is no need and thus no sufficient authority to require belief in anything beyond what Scripture requires. This is another basic Protestant principle designed to keep our focus on the gospel of Christ rather than on human ideas. May we always allow Scripture to accomplish its purpose of turning us toward Christ!

Roger L. Hahn is dean of the faculty and professor of New Testament at Nazarene Theological Seminary in Kansas City.

Word Study

Bible—from the Greek *biblos*, meaning "papyrus, book." Byblos was the ancient Phoenician city from which papyrus was exported.

Papyrus is a thin, paperlike material made from crushed and flattened stalks of a reedlike plant. The word "Bible" does not appear in the Scriptures.

Canon—from the Hebrew *qaneh* and the Greek *kanon*, both of which refer to a rule or measuring rod. The word "canon" comes from the rule of law that was used to determine which writings would comprise the biblical canon, or official Scripture. The books of the Old Testament were universally accepted at the time of Christ and were officially ratified by the Council of Jamnia in A.D. 90. The 27 books of the New Testament were officially recognized by Athanasius in the fourth century. The Council of Carthage in A.D. 397 confirmed these books and adopted their current order.

Gospel—from the Greek *euangelion* (also the origin of "evangelism") and Old English *godspel*, meaning "glad tidings" or "good news." The word was used in the New Testament to describe the message of Jesus. The first four books of the New Testament were called the gospels as early as the second century.

Testament—from the Late Latin *testamentum*, meaning "covenant." The Old Testament is the story of God's covenant with Abraham and his descendants, all of Israel. The New Testament is the gospel story of God's new covenant in Jesus Christ through the Cross to all humanity.

Fast Facts

The Old Testament was written in Hebrew and some Aramaic. The New Testament was written in Koine Greek.

By A.D. 600 the Catholic Church of Rome had restricted the Bible to only one language, Latin, used in the Vulgate.

John Wycliffe translated and produced the first handwritten English-language manuscript of the Bible in 1382.

The Bible was the first book ever printed. The Latin Vulgate Bible was printed in 1454 in Mainz, Germany, by Johannes Gutenberg, who invented the type mold for the printing press.

William Tyndale was the first to print the New Testament in the English language, in 1526.

A system of dividing the Scriptures into verses began as early as around A.D. 900, when Jewish scholars hand-copied the Bible. Following many earlier systems, modern chapter divisions were added in the 13th century. Since the Wycliffe English Bible of 1382, this pattern has been followed.

In 2000, 59 percent of Americans reported they read the Bible at least occasionally, and 37 percent said they read the Bible at least once a week. Beyond merely reading, only one in seven Americans, 14 percent, was involved in studying the Bible. (Alec Gallup and Wendy W. Simmons, "Six in Ten Americans Read Bible at Least Occasionally," The Gallup Organization, <www.gallup.com>, October 20, 2000.)

Quote Rack

As our society becomes increasingly pluralistic and subjective in its worldview, the more important it will be for Christians to know and study their Bibles. Only by doing so can we intelligently present a biblical worldview to a society that knows so little of the word that is able to save their souls.

—Michael J. Vlach, "Americans and the Bible"

Modern civilization is so complex as to make the devotional life all but impossible. It wears us out by multiplying distractions and beats us down destroying our solitude, where otherwise we might drink and renew our strength, before going out to face the world again. —A. W. Tozer, *Of God and Men*

It takes the same anointing to live the Bible as it did to write the Bible.

—V. H. Lewis
General Superintendent, 1960-1985

Scripture References

Luke 24:44-47; John 10:35; 1 Cor. 15:3-4; 2 Tim. 3:15-17; 1 Pet. 1:10-12; 2 Pet. 1:20-21.

5
SIN, ORIGINAL AND PERSONAL

We believe that sin came into the world through the disobedience of our first parents, and death by sin. We believe that sin is of two kinds: original sin or depravity, and actual or personal sin.

We believe that original sin, or depravity, is that corruption of the nature of all the offspring of Adam by reason of which everyone is very far gone from original righteousness or the pure state of our first parents at the time of their creation, is averse to God, is without spiritual life, and inclined to evil, and that continually. We further believe that original sin continues to exist with the new life of the regenerate, until the heart is fully cleansed by the baptism with the Holy Spirit.

We believe that original sin differs from actual sin in that it constitutes an inherited propensity to actual sin for which no one is accountable until its divinely provided remedy is neglected or rejected.

We believe that actual or personal sin is a voluntary violation of a known law of God by a morally responsible person. It is therefore not to be confused with involuntary and inescapable shortcomings, infirmities, faults, mistakes, failures, or other deviations from a standard of perfect conduct that are the residual effects of the Fall. However, such innocent effects do not include attitudes or responses contrary to the spirit of Christ, which may properly be called sins of the spirit. We believe that personal sin is primarily and essentially a violation of the law of love; and that in relation to Christ sin may be defined as unbelief.

—*Manual*, Article 5

The doctrine of original sin, says John Wesley, is "the first grand distinguishing point between Heathenism and Christianity." He then poses several questions: Are we "by nature filled with all manner of evil"? Are we "void of all good"? Are we "wholly fallen"? Are our souls "totally corrupted"? Is "every imagination of the thoughts of [our hearts] only evil continually"? "Allow this," says Wesley, "and you are so far a Christian. Deny it, and you are but an Heathen still" (*The Works of John Wesley*, 6:63).

Fallen in Adam, we are spiritually dead and morally corrupt and therefore unable of ourselves to turn to God and be saved. Only as the Spirit of God awakens and enables us—from the first awareness of our need until we stand before God in judgment—are we able to do one good deed; our salvation is only and entirely by His grace (Eph. 2:8-10).

Deprived of the sanctifying grace of God with which the race was originally endowed, we are born "curved in on ourselves," as Luther said. We have a serious curvature of the heart. Deprived of the Spirit, we are morally depraved. Sin is a racial fact before it is an individual act. Fallen in Adam, we inevitably "individuate" as sinners. In our own persons each of us reenacts the Fall. At some point in our personal journey—we call it the age of moral accountability—each of us hears God's voice within commanding, "Thou shalt not!" Without exception, because we are inwardly depraved, we inevitably disobey. It is thus that original sin becomes personal sin.

Such is our sinful predicament. "Explain it any way you choose," Professor Edward Ramsdell said in a divinity school lecture, "but you cannot explain it away—it is an empirical fact. It is not so much that we need it explained," he then added, "as that we need it resolved!" He was only echoing Wesley, who in closing his sermon "Original Sin" admonished, "Know your disease! Know your cure!" (*Works*, 6:65). Thank God, "A second Adam to the fight, and to the rescue came!" (John Henry Newman).

"Know your disease." It is twofold: We sin because we are sinners. Our redemption is therefore twofold: it is first pardon and then purity, through identification with Christ's death to sin. To embrace Him is to confess with the apostle Paul, "I have been crucified with Christ; and it is no longer I who live, but it is Christ who lives in me." He later adds, "Those who belong to Christ Jesus have crucified the flesh with its passions and desires" (Gal. 2:19-20; 5:24, NRSV). Crucifixion and death are two interrelated but distinct events. Jesus was crucified on Good Friday morning but did not die until that afternoon. And we are crucified with Him, says the apostle, "for the destruction of the sinful self" (Romans 6:6, REB).

"Know your cure." As God's grace begins to heal us, His first act is to pardon us from our sins and restore us to His favor. That miracle occurs when we repent of our sins and put our trust in Christ. In the very moment we are justified, we are "born from above" of the Holy Spirit. This initial miracle ends the reign of sin.

But sooner or later we discover that while sin's reign is broken, its root—lurking self-idolatry—remains. Love for God and others is real but mixed with sinful self-love. But God's purpose is deeper: We were crucified with Christ in order that we might die with Him and be made completely whole. (See Rom. 6:12-13, 19-22.)

The question is this: Have we truly died to sin and self? Dying is difficult, but die we must. "For the love of Christ urges us on," the apostle writes, "because we are convinced that one has died for all; therefore all have died. And he died for all, so that those who live might live no longer for themselves, but for him who died and was raised for them" (2 Cor. 5:14-15, NRSV). Our most desperate need is to be saved from ourselves! "We have met the enemy," said Pogo, "and he is us."

While death is not easy, by God's grace it is possible. We want a quick and easy death. It takes time, however, for God to reveal to us the depth of our need—and for us to die. The process cannot be hurried, so take time to come to the end of yourself. As He reveals, yield! When you are emptied of yourself, He will fill you with himself! "The one who calls you is faithful, and he will do this" (1 Thess. 5:24, NRSV).

William M. Greathouse is a general superintendent emeritus in the Church of the Nazarene.

Word Study

Sin—from the Indo-European root *es-*, meaning "to be." Like other words from this root, such as "essence," "is," "am," and "yes," sin in the Old English meant that which is real, true, and exists in the essence of being. We are born with a sinful nature (original sin), which leads us to commit acts of sin (personal sin).

John Wesley defined personal sin as "a voluntary transgression of a known law of God" (*The Letters of John Wesley, A.M.*, 5:322). For the single word "sin" in English used to identify personal acts of sin, more than one Greek word is used in the New Testament. Two of the most important are *anomia*, which means lawlessness or rebellion, and *hamartia*, which means falling short of the mark and may include mistakes as well as deliberate sins. When mistakes lead to "attitudes or responses contrary to the spirit of Christ" (*Manual*, Article 5), both *anomia* and *hamartia* are sins, and we should seek forgiveness for both.

Quote Rack

In prayer we are |often| not really much disturbed about |sin|; or, at least, not nearly so much as our heaped-up language would imply. What we imagine that we are achieving through this unreality I do not know. We shall not fool the All-wise; nor induce Him to believe that we are anything other, or better, than we actually are! Were it not saner to tell Him the truth, exactly as it is—not that we are overwhelmed with sorrow for our sinfulness, if it is not so; but rather this, that, to all our other sinfulness, we have added this last and crowning sinfulness, that we are not much worried about it, or, at least, not nearly as much as we ought to be. Be pleased, in pity, to grant us such measure of sorrow for our failures as will lead us to a true repentance; and, through that, to a new way of life.

—A. J. Gossip, *In the Secret Place of the Most High*

Ponder and Pursue

1. The Church of the Nazarene is an evangelical church, that is, we believe that each person can and must have a personal encounter with Jesus Christ to forgive sins. Why is this necessary? (Rom. 3:23; 6:23). What is the result of forgiveness of sins? (John 3:16; John 8:34-36; Gal. 4:4-7; Titus 3:4-7)

2. How does Paul describe the distress of one who has turned from sin but is now trying to be righteous by his or her own efforts and by keeping the law? (Rom. 7:15-24). Such a person is "at war" (v. 23, NRSV) within—trying to be good but unable to do so on his own.

3. After we are forgiven of our personal acts of sin, what is the solution to the inner nature of sin? (Rom. 8). What does it mean to live according to the Spirit? (See also chapter 10: Entire Sanctification.)

4. Through the power of the Holy Spirit (Acts 1:8), we can live above sin. What does Rom. 6 say about continuing in sin? Note Paul's emphatic declaration in verses 2 and 15.

Additional Scripture References

Original sin: Gen. 3; 6:5; Job 15:14; Ps. 51:5; Jer. 17:9-10; Mark 7:21-23; Rom. 1:18-25; 5:12-14; 7:1—8:9; 1 Cor. 3:1-4; Gal. 5:16-25; 1 John 1:7-8.

Personal sin: Matt. 22:36-40 (with 1 John 3:4); John 16:8-9; Rom. 6:15-23; 8:18-24; 14:23; 1 John 1:9—2:4; 3:7-10.

6
ATONEMENT

We believe that Jesus Christ, by His sufferings, by the shedding of His own blood, and by His death on the Cross, made a full atonement for all human sin, and that this Atonement is the only ground of salvation, and that it is sufficient for every individual of Adam's race. The Atonement is graciously efficacious for the salvation of the irresponsible and for the children in innocency but is efficacious for the salvation of those who reach the age of responsibility only when they repent and believe.

—*Manual*, Article 6

William Tyndale, the famed Bible translator, first coined the English word "atonement" to mean "at-one-ment," the reconciling of two to be "at one." Today we use the word for the whole doctrine of how salvation comes through the death of Christ. But to understand this great doctrine, we need to remember five things:

- The death of our Lord Jesus Christ cannot be understood at all apart from His incarnation. What He did for us on the Cross is understood in the light of who He is —the God-man.
- The Atonement is a mystery we can never fully understand. Older textbooks referred to "theories" of the Atonement, but actually there is no such thing. Not one of the so-called theories can explain the Atonement.

38

- To understand the mystery as much as we are able, we need every one of the models and metaphors in holy Scripture.
- The Atonement was first corporate, for the whole human race, and so may become personal—"for me"—through faith.
- The Atonement is the source not only of our justification or pardon but also of our sanctification.

With these points in mind, we begin then with Christ.

1. Christ is our victorious King. Just as the Lord God triumphed over the gods of Egypt and redeemed Israel from slavery at the Exodus, so God in Christ triumphed over all the forces of evil (Col. 2:15). In His kingly victory, proclaimed in His resurrection, Jesus our Lord revealed His true deity and His authority over death and hell.

The implication, as William Greathouse has argued, is that each redeemed Christian shares in that victory over sin already—today—in advance of the final victory of the Last Day.

2. Christ is our High Priest. He has become human (Heb. 2:14-18), and only because He is truly one of us can He represent us to God.

Here we come to the second meaning of the English word "atonement": the act of the Old Testament priest in offering to God a sacrifice for sin to avert God's judgment. The modern mind finds the idea of coming judgment offensive, but that judgment is precisely why we need a priest and advocate.

Unlike ancient pagan priests, however, the Old Testament priest did not offer some innocent victim to appease the anger of reluctant gods. Rather, God took the initiative by providing the sacrificial system and appointing the priests. And so in Christ, God's love took the initiative. But in Christ, His initiative is astounding! For unlike the sacrifices of Israel, Christ was not only the Priest but also simultaneously the sacrifice. The Priest was also the Lamb! He offered himself to God, a voluntary self-sacrifice.

But God's initiative is yet more astounding. In the light of His deity, we see that it was God Incarnate who suffered for us. God Incarnate "bore our sins in His own body on the tree" (1 Pet. 2:24, NKJV). Far from being the unjust punishment of an innocent third party, this was the highest conceivable ethical act. God Incarnate took on himself the consequences of our sin. Far from the wringing of a reluctant pardon from an angry God, this was the love of God cutting through wrath and judgment to satisfy not only His own justice but also His love. Here in Christ is corporate at-one-ment for all of Adam's sinful race, including therefore "the irresponsible and . . . children in innocency," (*Manual*, Article 6).

And there's more. Reconciliation to a holy God required obliteration of the offensive sin. The Cross had to effect pardon for acts of sin and also deal with original sin. Somehow the crucifixion of the sinless Lamb of God effected the death of the old corporate, sinful, Adamic humanity (Rom. 6:6-10). The Lamb-Priest provides the cleansing of all sin for all humanity once and for all. Only so may each believer then die to sin within.

3. Christ is our Prophet. He reveals to us the heart of God. The Old Testament prophets spoke the word of the Lord, but Christ is the Word of the Lord, the Word made flesh. Deity and humanity are forever at one in the unity of the Person of the God-man.

Not just in Christ's teaching but also supremely in His cross we see the loving heart of God (Rom. 5:8). How much does God love us? Enough to become one of us—a human being, condemned, rejected, humiliated, plumbing the depths of human agony and degradation, abandoned to death even by His God (Mark 15:34). As we see such love, God the Holy Spirit inspires us to respond in faith, so that we may love God as He has loved us. Perfect love is the fruit of the Atonement. Therefore, out of cosmic and corporate at-one-ment comes the personal forgiveness and reconciliation to God of those who believe. In Christ we are "at one" with God.

Thomas A. Noble is professor of theology at Nazarene Theological Seminary in Kansas City and supervises Ph.D. students at Nazarene Theological College in Manchester, England.

Word Study

Atonement—from the Middle English *atonen*, meaning "to be reconciled" or become "at one." Though the meanings "to agree" and "to harmonize" are now listed as archaic or obsolete, these connotations hold special significance for the Christian. Through the redemptive life and death of Jesus Christ, God and humanity are reconciled, brought into agreement and harmony.

Quote Rack

A man can no more repent than he can do anything else without a motive; and the motive which makes evangelical repentance possible does not enter into his world till he sees God as God makes himself known in the death of Christ. All true penitents are children of the Cross. Their penitence is not their own creation: it is the reaction towards God produced in their souls by this demonstration of what sin is to Him, and of what His love does to reach and win the sinful.

—James Denney, *The Atonement and the Modern Mind*

Witnesses to the Faith

When Hannes first visited First Church of the Nazarene in Frankfurt, Germany, everything was new to him. He continued to come every week, confessing to Pastor Hans Zimmerman, "I need more time to understand." One Sunday morning the Holy Spirit broke through to his heart. Although Hannes had witnessed people going forward and kneeling at the altar at the pastor's invitation to receive Christ as Savior, Hannes responded differently. He left his seat and walked slowly—not to the altar but to a side wall where a large cross hung. He stood before the cross, his mouth moving but no words audible. When the pastor approached to pray with him, Hannes responded, "Thank you. Just give me some more time. There is so much I need to straighten out." The Holy Spirit had spoken to Hannes, drawing him to the cross. In that sanctuary, the physical representation of Christ's death became the place Hannes found forgiveness and became "at one" with God.

Ponder and Pursue

1. The Old Testament prophecies regarding the Messiah indicated He would die a voluntary death as a sacrifice for all. Read Isa. 53:1-12. Make a list of the characteristics of the suffering Messiah found in these verses.

2. The New Testament records the fulfillment of Old Testament prophecies in Jesus Christ as the One who made atonement by laying down His life. Read the words of Christ in Matt. 20:28 and John 10:7-18 and Peter's words about Him in 1 Pet. 2:23-25. How do these verses directly correlate with Isaiah's prophecy?

Additional Scripture References

Mark 10:45; Luke 24:46-48; John 1:29; 3:14-17; Acts 4:10-12; Rom. 3:21-26; 4:17-25; 5:6-21; 1 Cor. 6:20; 2 Cor. 5:14-21; Gal. 1:3-4; 3:13-14; Col. 1:19-23; 1 Tim. 2:3-6; Titus 2:11-14; Heb. 2:9; 9:11-14; 13:12; 1 Pet. 1:18-21; 2:19-25; 1 John 2:1-2.

7
PREVENIENT GRACE

We believe that the human race's creation in God-likeness included ability to choose between right and wrong, and that thus human beings were made morally responsible; that through the fall of Adam they became depraved so that they cannot now turn and prepare themselves by their own natural strength and works to faith and calling upon God. But we also believe that the grace of God through Jesus Christ is freely bestowed upon all people, enabling all who will to turn from sin to righteousness, believe on Jesus Christ for pardon and cleansing from sin, and follow good works pleasing and acceptable in His sight.

We believe that all persons, though in the possession of the experience of regeneration and entire sanctification, may fall from grace and apostatize and, unless they repent of their sins, be hopelessly and eternally lost.

—Manual, Article 7

Volodymyr ("Vova") Masyuk pastors First Church of the Nazarene in Kyiv, Ukraine. Nothing in his childhood suggested he would heed such a call. When Vova was 10, his father, a member of the Ukrainian Communist Party, gave him *A Book for a Young Atheist.* Although it seemed likely he would fulfill his father's hopes and embrace atheism and Communism, Vova traces the subtle movements of God's grace that brought him to salvation instead.

Before Vova began elementary school, another child reported his own Christian baptism. Vova told the boy that myths had deceived him. At age 13, Vova and some friends harassed an elderly Orthodox woman as she left church. She shook Vova's atheistic confidence by warning, "God can rain down rocks on your head." *Could God do that?* Vova wondered. Later, in a rebellious mood, he listened to Western rock music. As he heard *Jesus Christ Superstar,* he thought, *How could Jesus attract the attention of so many young people in America?* About that time, someone gave Vova a book about the life of Jesus. He tried to discuss its "legends" with a friend, whose response rattled him: "Vova, those stories are true." More awakening followed. When Mikhail Gorbachev was Communist Party general secretary (1985-1991), a window for Christian evangelism opened. Out of curiosity, Vova went to hear an Episcopalian evangelist. During the sermon the Holy Spirit called Vova to repentance and confession of faith in Jesus Christ.

Vova's story illustrates what the Church of the Nazarene means by prevenient grace. Though not unique to the Wesleyan tradition, it is pivotal to our understanding of God, grace, and salvation.

First, the atonement for sins Jesus made on the Cross was accomplished for all persons. God is not willing that any should perish but that all should come to repentance and eternal life (John 3:16; 2 Pet. 3:9).

Second, as the incarnate mediator between God and humanity, Christ is the author of grace (Rom. 1:5; 3:24). God's creative and redemptive acts occur at the will of the Father, through the Son, and by the agency of the Holy Spirit. While we correctly say that God is gracious, we must add "through the mediation of His Son." The New Testament tells us the

Father creates and redeems through His Son (Col. 1:16; Heb. 1:2; 1 Cor. 1:30). He is and always has been the one mediator between God and humanity (John 8:56-58; 1 Cor. 10:1-5; 1 Pet. 1:10-12). The Old Testament economy of salvation anticipated a fulfillment in Christ. He underwrote its redemptive quality. Therefore we say that all grace is of Christ.

Third, all grace has conversion and sanctification as its goal. Wherever God reaches humanity, He does so looking toward reconciliation. All grace is the work of Christ, whose purpose on Calvary was to reconcile all persons to God.

Fourth, no person is a stranger to God's grace. Long before we are aware of God's activity in our lives, and long before we hear the gospel proclaimed, Christ through the Spirit is active. He works to lead all persons to conversion and creates the conditions for conversion to occur. A human messenger who declares the gospel speaks not in a religious vacuum but where the Spirit has prepared the way.

The Spirit of God awakens our most elementary religious sensitivities, quickening our conscience to the reality of God. Were God to leave us alone in our sins, we would not even think about Him. The Spirit begins to press God's claims on us. Far from being natural, the conscience results from the Spirit's activity. Our capacity to know right from wrong and our sense that moral responsibility is essential to our humanity is the Spirit's doing. The specific commands of the conscience come from many sources and need correction by the Holy Spirit. He restores the freedom of the will, setting it free for God. Otherwise, our wills would remain bound in sin. In His prevenient work, the Spirit removes the guilt associated with original sin so that no person stands guilty for Adam's sin. In sum, void of God's gracious efforts to redeem, the "natural man" is an abstraction.

God works in astonishing ways to draw persons to salvation. We can have confidence in His ways and become instruments of His grace. Because grace is the work of the sovereign God, no one should try to limit the extent to which persons might respond prior to a transforming encounter with Christ. The Church plays an important role in the movements of grace. The Church should pray that in its ministries it will serve God by cultivating prevenient grace.

Al Truesdale is professor emeritus of philosophy of religion and Christian ethics at Nazarene Theological Seminary, in Kansas City.

Word Study

Prevenient—from the Indo-European root *gwā*, meaning "to come," prevenient belongs to a family of "coming" words, including "advent," "avenue," "convention," and "covenant." Just as "intervene" means "to come between," "prevenient" with its prefix *pre-* means "coming before." God's prevenient grace is His gracious activity in our lives long before we hear the gospel proclaimed.

Grace—from the Indo-European root *gwerə-2*, meaning "to favor," grace is mercy, clemency, a favor rendered by one who needs not do so. The Greek word in the New Testament translated "grace" is *charis*, closely related to *chrisma*, meaning "gift." God's grace is His unmerited gift of favor to humanity. Like grace's sister word "gratis," His grace is freely bestowed on those who do not deserve it and cannot earn it.

Witnesses to the Faith

In the rugged, mountainous country surrounded entirely by the Republic of South Africa sits the country of Lesotho. Sometimes called the Switzerland of South Africa because of its beautiful scenery, Lesotho is a poor country with only a few manufacturing industries. Most of Lesotho's people are Black Africans called Basotho, and the women are largely responsible for the heavy work on the farms and in the homes. Unreached people groups, those who have never heard the gospel, live in Lesotho's remote areas, inaccessible to all except the most determined by horseback, arduous driving, or flight on a small plane. Nazarene missionary Dale Stotler braved the grueling journey. Following his preaching, many repented and believed. Though she had just heard of Christ for the first time, one new convert told Rev. Stotler, "I dreamed of a man of fair complexion who would come and tell us about a man whose name was Jesus. You are that messenger." God's prevenient grace goes before us in ways that we cannot understand, His mysteries reaching all cultures. His grace is still amazing.

Quote Rack

> *Justice and Judgment are thy throne*
> *Yet wondrous is thy grace;*
> *While truth and mercy joined in one,*
> *Invite us near thy face.*
>
> —Isaac Watts

Grace is the incomprehensible fact that God is well pleased with a man, and that a man can rejoice in God. Only when grace is recognized to be incomprehensible is it grace. . . . Grace is the gift of Christ, who exposes the gulf which separates God and man, and, by exposing it, bridges it. —Karl Barth, *The Epistle to the Romans*

Ponder and Pursue

1. How does being made in the likeness of God make us morally responsible for choosing between right and wrong? Read Gen. 1:26-27; 2:16-17. How are free will and grace intertwined in God's redemptive plan? Read Josh. 24:14-18.

2. Jesus said, "No one can come to me unless the Father who sent me draws him" (John 6:44). How are the Father, Son, and Holy Spirit active together in prevenient grace? Read John 16:13; Rom. 5:6-11; 1 Cor. 2:9-10; and Heb. 9:14.

3. In what way did you feel God drawing you before you came to know Christ as Savior? How can the Church be a channel through which God's prevenient grace might flow?

Additional Scripture References

Godlikeness and moral responsibility: Deut. 28:1-2; 30:19; Ps. 8:3-5; Isa. 1:8-10; Jer. 31:29-30; Ezek. 18:1-4; Mic. 6:8; Rom. 1:19-20; 2:1-16; 14:7-12; Gal. 6:7-8.

Natural inability: Job 14:4; 15:14; Ps. 14:1-4; 51:5; John 3:6; Rom. 3:10-12; 5:12-14, 20; 7:14-25.

Free grace and works of faith: Ezek. 18:25-26; John 1:12-13; 3:6; Acts 5:31; Rom. 5:18; 6:15-16, 23; 10:6-8; 11:22; 1 Cor. 2:9-14; 10:1-12; 2 Cor. 5:18-19; Gal. 5:6; Eph. 2:8-10; Phil. 2:12-13; Col. 1:21-23; 2 Tim. 4:10; Titus 2:11-14; Heb. 2:1-3; 3:12-15; 6:4-6; 10:26-31; James 2:18-22; 2 Pet. 1:10-11; 2:20-22.

8
REPENTANCE

We believe that repentance, which is a sincere and thorough change of the mind in regard to sin, involving a sense of personal guilt and a voluntary turning away from sin, is demanded of all who have by act or purpose become sinners against God. The Spirit of God gives to all who will repent the gracious help of penitence of heart and hope of mercy, that they may believe unto pardon and spiritual life.

—*Manual*, Article 8

In the Bible, "repent" most simply means "turn around." The implication is that a person who repents turns away from a life of sin and idolatry and toward the gracious love and will of God.

Israel's prophets preached God's calling upon the people to repent from their disobedience and idolatry and turn back with humble and grateful hearts to God, who covenanted with them at Mount Sinai (Exod. 20). David penned his great song of repentance in deep remorse for his adulterous relationship with Bathsheba. "According to the greatness of Your compassion blot out my transgressions," David cried. "Wash me thoroughly from my iniquity And cleanse me from my sin" (Ps. 51:1-2, NASB).

Given the importance of the theme of Israel's need for repentance throughout the writings of the Hebrew prophets, it is not surprising that repentance was the heart of John the

Baptist's preaching. According to Mark, John proclaimed "a baptism of repentance for the forgiveness of sins" (Mark 1:4). Matthew recorded identical summaries of the preaching of John and Jesus: "Repent, for the kingdom of heaven is at hand" (Matt. 3:2; 4:17, NASB).

The fact that both John the Baptist and Jesus the Nazarene connected repentance with the coming of God's kingdom is highly significant. This connection helps us understand the unique nature of repentance in New Testament teaching. Human beings are called to turn around, reorient their hearts and lives, and live in a radically new way in the light of the kingdom Jesus introduced into the world.

Matthew recorded a marvelous illustration of this call. Some Pharisees accused Jesus of performing mighty deeds by the power of "Beelzebul the ruler of the demons" (Matt. 12:24, NASB). Jesus replied, "If I cast out demons by the Spirit of God, then the kingdom of God has come upon you" (v. 28, NASB). In other words, Jesus' ministry of preaching, teaching, healing, and deliverance was a demonstration of the presence and power of God's Spirit. Thus, in Jesus' own person and work God's kingdom invaded and began to redeem our fallen world. In the presence of Jesus, in the transforming power of the Spirit, we are beckoned to turn from our selfish, wicked ways and greet the coming of the Kingdom. God's always-coming kingdom demands change!

We should note, too, that Jesus warned His accusers that "whoever speaks against the Holy Spirit, it shall not be forgiven him, either in this age or in the age to come" (Matt. 12:32, NASB). By giving the prince of darkness credit for Jesus' power to exorcise and heal, the Pharisees were in serious danger of speaking against (or blaspheming) the Holy Spirit, who was laboring mightily in and through our Lord. The *Manual* article on repentance states that "the Spirit of God gives to all who will repent the gracious help of penitence of heart and hope of mercy," but we see in this gospel story an example of how this gracious help can be forfeited. Those who opposed Jesus were resisting the very presence and power of the Spirit of God and were, in essence, calling good evil. Should one persist in calling good evil or evil good (as in Gen. 3:6), the heart can become so hardened that there is no desire to repent. Those who persistently resist the Spirit steel themselves against God's loving mercy in this present age and also in God's age to come.

The New Testament, then, teaches us that Jesus' coming into the world has brought about a brand-new situation in which all human beings are called to turn around. Before Jesus' coming, God "overlooked the times of ignorance, [but He] is now declaring . . . that all people everywhere should repent" (Acts 17:30, NASB). We are required to repent, or turn around, because the coming of God's kingdom into the world through Jesus Christ demands faithful subjects.

Paul rejoiced that the Thessalonians "turned to God from idols to serve the living and true God" (1 Thess. 1:9). So repenting does not simply mean feeling sorry for the sins we have committed but involves an actual, practical turning-around of our lives. No wonder John told his listeners, "Bear fruits in keeping with repentance" (Luke 3:8, NASB), and Jesus told the adulterous woman, "From now on sin no more" (John 8:11, NASB).

Finally, it is important to see that while repentance is a human act, it is not accomplished simply or only by us. Even in our "voluntary turning away from sin" (*Manual*, Article 8), we stand in deep need of divine help. Though God cannot— or at least does not—force us to repent, it is His kindness that leads us to repentance (Rom. 2:4, NASB), and it is He who grants repentance (Acts 5:31). Thus, believing that "the Spirit of God gives to all who will repent the gracious help of penitence of heart and hope of mercy" (*Manual*, Article 8), we are confident that even while we are turning, God is already enabling us to do so through the empowering of the Holy Spirit.

Michael E. Lodahl is professor of theology at Point Loma Nazarene University, in San Diego.

Word Study

Repent—from the Latin *paenitēre*, for "to be sorry." Most are familiar with repentance as godly sorrow for sin. However, the definition goes further. The Greek word translated "repentance" in the New Testament is *metanoia*, which includes a change of mind, a complete turning around. To repent is to feel such regret for past conduct as to change one's mind and behavior. The Indo-European root *pent-* means "to tread," the source of the English words "path" and "footpad." In true repentance, we are not only sorry; we also turn away from sin, change direction, and tread a new path.

Witnesses to the Faith

Janis found turning 21 a thrill. Alcohol was now legal, even though she had already started drinking as a teen. "Add that to my bad language," Janis says now, "and my life was in trouble." Her mother's faithful prayers for her salvation were considered a threat to her pleasures, and Janis's words to her cut like knives. But after she was married, God revealed her sinful life to her. "For four long hours God reminded me of all the sins I had committed, and in the midst of the battle, I repented." God's gracious salvation prompted her through many tears to ask forgiveness of her mother, her husband, and her children. She turned from her sins but found that God allowed her to keep and use her personality in new ways. After 55 years of living for Christ, she says, "My bold personality is still the same today, but my character has changed to honor God." According to Janis, turning from a life of sin is still a thrill at age 80.

Quote Rack

Repentance is in every view so desirable, so necessary, so suited to honor God, that I seek that above all. The tender heart, the broken and contrite spirit, are to me far above all the joys that I could ever hope for in this vale of tears. I long to be in my proper place, my hand on my mouth, and my mouth in the dust . . . I feel this to be safe ground. Here I cannot err . . . I am sure that whatever God may despise . . . He will not despise the broken and contrite heart.
—Charles Simeon

Ponder and Pursue

Both Saul and David were chosen by God as king of Israel. Both disobeyed God (Saul: 1 Sam. 15:1-9; David: 2 Sam. 11). Both were confronted about their sins (Saul: 1 Sam. 15:10-23; David: 2 Sam. 12:1-12). But here their similarities end.

1. How do the responses of Saul and David to their sin differ? (1 Sam. 15:24-30; 2 Sam. 12:13; Ps. 51).

2. Examine again the definition of repentance and then the responses of Saul and David. What is the difference between sorrow for sin and complete repentance? What was Saul's main motivation in asking forgiveness? (1 Sam. 15:30). What was David's? (Ps. 51).

3. How did their responses directly affect their reigns, the rest of their lives, and ultimately the entire nation of Israel? (Saul: 1 Sam. 15:10-11, 23, 35; 31:1-13; David: 2 Sam. 22:21-25, 51; 23:3-5).

4. Scripture suggests that the "turning" of true repentance will affect multiple aspects of our lives:

Our thinking—Isa. 55:6-7; Rom. 8:5-9; 12:1-2

Our pleasures—Eph. 5:8-10

Our appetites—1 Pet. 2:2

Our goals—Matt. 6:32-33; Col. 3:1-2

Our desires—Rom. 13:14; Gal. 5:16; 1 John 2:15-17

The object of our eyes—Ps. 101:3; Matt. 5:28-29; Heb. 12:2

Additional Scripture References

2 Chron. 7:14; Ps. 32:5-6; Jer. 3:12-14; Ezek. 18:30-32; 33:14-16; Mark 1:14-15; Luke 3:1-14; 13:1-5; 18:9-14; Acts 2:38; 3:19; 5:31; 17:30-31; 26:16-18; Rom. 2:4; 2 Cor. 7:8-11; 1 Thess. 1:9; 2 Pet. 3:9.

9

JUSTIFICATION, REGENERATION, AND ADOPTION

We believe that justification is the gracious and judicial act of God by which He grants full pardon of all guilt and complete release from the penalty of sins committed, and acceptance as righteous, to all who believe on Jesus Christ and receive Him as Lord and Savior.

We believe that regeneration, or the new birth, is that gracious work of God whereby the moral nature of the repentant believer is spiritually quickened and given a distinctively spiritual life, capable of faith, love, and obedience.

We believe that adoption is that gracious act of God by which the justified and regenerated believer is constituted a son of God.

We believe that justification, regeneration, and adoption are simultaneous in the experience of seekers after God and are obtained upon the condition of faith, preceded by repentance; and that to this work and state of grace the Holy Spirit bears witness.

—*Manual*, Article 9

The three terms in the title of the ninth article of faith describe some of the benefits available from a right relationship with God. These benefits exist because God acts first, or preveniently, to offer them to us. We are justified, regenerated, and adopted when we cooperate by responding appropriately to God.

Justification, regeneration, and adoption are not three discrete states that we experience in chronological order. Rather, the three intertwine and interrelate. Together they express important ideas about our ongoing relationship with God.

Let's begin with adoption. Having wise and loving parents is a privilege many of us enjoy. But even the wisest and most loving parents do not nurture children perfectly. In fact, perfect human parents do not exist.

To accept adoption by God, however, is to enter into a parent-child relationship of a different kind. In God we find the perfect love and wisdom of the perfect Parent.

This Parent not only acts perfectly but also continually invites everyone to join the family of faith. Joining this family means becoming a coheir with our Brother and Savior, Jesus, and with others who accept their adoption.

The process of adopting a child today differs somewhat from the process familiar to the original writers and readers of Scripture. Today we most often adopt babies or very young children. Because of their age, these little ones have no real say in the process.

By contrast, those in ancient times thought of adoption as the act of offering older children, young teens, and young adults the benefits of family assistance and prestige. Those who were offered the advantages of adoption could accept or reject. Accepting meant assuming a new name. It also meant cutting ties to other familial associations.

These two adoption customs point to an important aspect of the theology of the Church of the Nazarene. We do not think of adoption as God forcing conditions upon us against our will. Our adoption is not coercive. Rather, we think of God offering to adopt us. And this offer awaits our free response.

When we accept adoption, we are likely to join John in saying, "How great is the love the Father has lavished on us, that we should be called children of God!" (1 John 3:1).

The idea of adoption leads naturally to the idea that Christians start a new life and take on a new identity. Perhaps the best word for this change is "regeneration."

If you have ever aspired to begin life anew, you have wanted to be regenerated. When we accept our adoption and live as children of God, we enter into a lifelong adventure in transformation—or as the apostle Paul puts it, we are new creations (2 Cor. 5:17).

Sometimes people speak as though regeneration occurs only early in the life of faith. Some think of being "born again" as something that happens once, only sometime in the past.

The theology that informs the Church of the Nazarene, however, considers regeneration an ongoing occurrence. Although in some ways we become instantaneously new when we begin our adventure in faith, God continually offers new ways to experience the abundant life of regeneration.

We might best conceive of regeneration by comparing it to the healing that occurs after we've been injured. Just as cells, skin, and other parts of our bodies regenerate as they heal, so we might think of the Christian life as a regenerative process of recovery from the habits and injury of sin. And that's an ongoing process.

Christian regeneration affects many aspects of life. One of the most distinctive changes comes in our moral judgments. Because God enlivens our sense of right and wrong, we develop a clearer sense of how to live life to the fullest.

Of course, to say we have an enlivened sense of right and wrong does not mean we always know with absolute certainty which actions are righteous and which actions are not. Believers can come to differing opinions about some moral questions. Despite these differences, however, we can rest assured that God quickens our moral senses so we might better discern the ways of virtue. Living in the family of faith helps hone these skills of discernment.

The first term listed in the ninth article of faith is justification. Christians historically have often understood justification in legal terms.

Legally, justification represents God's pardon and release from penalty. God neither deems us guilty nor punishes us for sins we have committed. However, we may continue to deal with some of the natural negative consequences of sin.

Adoptions require official witnesses. And the miracle of regenerative healing carries greater weight when others—particularly physicians—officially recognize it. The legal connotation of justification reminds us that our adoption and regeneration are legitimate. The Spirit "testifies" (NIV) or "bears witness" (NKJV) that we are God's children (Rom. 8:16). And that's worth celebrating!

Thomas Jay Oord is professor of theology and philosophy at Northwest Nazarene University, in Nampa, Idaho.

Word Study

Justification—from the Indo-European root *yewes-*, meaning "law," the source of many legal words in English, such as "jury," "jurisdiction," "perjure," and "just." Justification is the act of proving to be just or right, or absolving of blame. A righteous, just God justifies us, freeing us by grace from the guilt of sin as measured by the law.

Regeneration—from the Indo-European root *genə*—meaning "to give birth," the source for "generation," "gender," and "indigenous." With its prefix "re-," to be regenerated is to be born again, a spiritual rebirth.

Adoption—from the Latin *adoptā, ad- + optāre*, meaning "to choose." To adopt is to take into a family by legal means and raise as one's own child. God has chosen us to be His children.

Quote Rack

Peace comes when there is no cloud between us and God. Peace is the consequence of forgiveness, God's removal of that which obscures His face and so breaks union with Him. The happy sequence culminating in fellowship with God is penitence, pardon, and peace—the first we offer, the second we accept, and the third we inherit. —Charles H. Brent

Witnesses to the Faith

In 1999 Michael was without hope. After a life of emotional illness brought him to the brink of suicide, he was committed to a hospital and then rehabilitation. Upon release, he thought he had his life together, even becoming a counselor to others. But deep within, he knew something was missing, and soon he found himself back in rehabilitation. There had to be a better way than the medications his doctor said he would need in order to live a manageable life. He needed a greater help. His search led him to the Church of the Nazarene. The pastor encouraged Michael to look not to his own problems or pain but to Christ, who died for our sins and bore our pain. Together they prayed the sinner's prayer, and Michael became a new creation in Christ. Now a child of God, he began a new future that included restored relationships with his earthly family. Today Michael leads two discipleship classes in an effort to show others the way to a new life through Jesus Christ.

Ponder and Pursue

1. In John 3:3-21, Jesus explains regeneration to Nicodemus. What is the difference between being born of the flesh and being born of the Spirit (v. 6)? From whom does this new Spirit life come (v. 6)? Jesus also uses several "legal" words throughout verses 10-21, including "testify," "testimony," and "verdict." Considering the word studies for this chapter, how did Jesus' language help this teacher of the law understand both justification and regeneration?

2. In John 5:24, Jesus again links justification with regeneration. Which words of this verse apply specifically to justification, and which to regeneration?

3. Read Rom. 8:13-17. What does it mean to live in the "Spirit of sonship" (v. 15)?

4. Rom. 3:21-26 beautifully weaves together the doctrines of Article 5: Sin, Original and Personal (v. 23); Article 6: Atonement (vv. 24-25); Article 7: Prevenient Grace (v. 24); and Article 9: Justification, Regeneration, and Adoption (vv. 24-26). As you read, circle these words: "righteousness," "justified," "justice," "just." According

58 ARTICLES OF FAITH

to Rom. 3 and 4, what is the condition upon which justification is
obtained (3:28)?

Additional Scripture References

Luke 18:14; John 1:12-13; Acts 13:39; Rom. 1:17; 4:5-9, 17-25; 5:1,
16-19; 6:4; 7:6; 8:1; 1 Cor. 1:30; 6:11; 2 Cor. 5:17-21; Gal. 2:16-21; 3:1-
14, 26; 4:4-7; Eph. 1:6-7; 2:1, 4-5; Phil. 3:3-9; Col. 2:13; Titus 3:4-7; 1
Pet. 1:23; 1 John 1:9; 3:1-2, 9; 4:7; 5:1, 9-13, 18.

10
ENTIRE SANCTIFICATION

We believe that entire sanctification is that act of God, subsequent to regeneration, by which believers are made free from original sin, or depravity, and brought into a state of entire devotement to God, and the holy obedience of love made perfect.

It is wrought by the baptism with the Holy Spirit, and comprehends in one experience the cleansing of the heart from sin and the abiding, indwelling presence of the Holy Spirit, empowering the believer for life and service.

Entire sanctification is provided by the blood of Jesus, is wrought instantaneously by faith, preceded by entire consecration; and to this work and state of grace the Holy Spirit bears witness.

This experience is also known by various terms representing its different phases, such as "Christian perfection," "perfect love," "heart purity," "the baptism with the Holy Spirit," "the fullness of the blessing," and "Christian holiness."

We believe that there is a marked distinction between a pure heart and a mature character. The former is obtained in an instant, the result of entire sanctification; the latter is the result of growth in grace.

We believe that the grace of entire sanctification includes the impulse to grow in grace. However, this impulse must be consciously nurtured, and careful attention given to the requisites and processes of spiritual development and improvement in Christlikeness of character and personality. Without such purposeful endeavor, one's witness may be impaired and the grace itself frustrated and ultimately lost.

—*Manual*, Article 10

justification — when we accept Christ

sanctification — The work of a lifetime — christian maturing.

To be converted to Christ is to be set on the road to moral and spiritual wholeness—in other words, to a life of holiness. Within this life process, a distinctive moment is possible that cleanses the believer from original sin and brings entire devotement to God. This "crisis" moment, an identifiable point in time, is known as entire sanctification.

We believe Christ's redemption, including holiness broadly conceived and entire sanctification, is totally adequate to meet humanity's deepest need. The atonement of Christ deals not only with the works or manifestations of sin—with sins and sinning—but also with the condition of sin, or in other words, not only with the symptoms but also with the disease itself. With the apostle Paul we exult, "Where sin abounded, grace did much more abound" (Rom. 5:20, KJV).

Salvation in Christ means deliverance from sin (Matt. 1:21). In justification we are delivered from the past, or guilt of sin. Simultaneously, in regeneration (new birth) we are delivered from the power of sin. In entire sanctification we are delivered from the pollution of sin. In glorification we will be delivered from the presence and effects of sin. At every stage of salvation, we are being delivered or saved continuously, moment by moment.

From the beautiful and balanced statement of Article 10 come the following highlighted affirmations.

1. Entire sanctification is an act of God. Like all stages of salvation, sanctification is by grace through faith in Jesus Christ. It does not occur as a result of one's efforts, no matter how worthy or altruistic. One is not sanctified "wholly" either because of one's merits or by one's good deeds. Acts of compassion done "in the name of Christ" flow out of God's gracious activity in the heart and do not accrue merit to receive the grace of sanctification.

Entire sanctification generally occurs "subsequent to regeneration" (*Manual*, Article 10). Scripture suggests some kind of "secondness" in Christian experience, as for example in the entire epistle of 1 Thess. (see 5:23-24). Further, following their conversion, believers eventually come to a point of increasing awareness of a spirit that is unfriendly to godliness. They are confronted with a strong propensity to self-sovereignty and the gratification of self-will.

Virtually all evangelical Christians acknowledge that holiness or sanctification is taught in the Bible and that it brings believers freedom from sin through the merits of Christ's death. There is widespread disagreement, however, regarding the meaning of freedom from sin and when it becomes an actuality in the believer.

Four different views have been commonly expressed:

- *Holiness (entire sanctification) is simultaneous with regeneration and is completed then.* This view is contrary to universal Christian experience. Regenerate persons of every era have acknowledged the antagonisms to divine love they discover within themselves under the illumination of the Holy Spirit. Believers have been so strongly aware of the perverse tendencies of their own natures that many have concluded there can be no deliverance until, or perhaps by the means of, purgatorial fires. Further, the view that holiness is completed in conversion contradicts the creed of all the orthodox branches of the Church.
- *Holiness is a matter of spiritual growth from regeneration until physical death.*

- *Persons are made holy in the moment of death.* Christian experience fails to confirm the views that holiness is by growth or death. No one claims to have grown into a spiritual state of complete deliverance from the tyranny of a sinful self, nor are there grounds in the Scriptures for these views.

The fourth view of holiness is the one Nazarenes believe:

- *Holiness is begun in regeneration, is continued by a further instantaneous work of heart cleansing (entire sanctification) wrought by the Holy Spirit "subsequent to regeneration," and progresses throughout the life of the believer to glorification.*

The question may be raised as to why there are two works of grace. Perhaps the best response is that there are levels of awareness of need. Nonbelievers cannot know the depth of their sinful condition and selfish depravity until they begin to walk with the Lord and experience His holiness (see Isa. 6).

The testimonies of others outside the Holiness Movement to a second work seem to corroborate the witness of Scripture and experience. Earlier Holiness exponents underscored "secondness" over the theory that one is made holy by growth or by death.

A believer is not only cleansed from original sin, the spirit of self-sovereignty that tends to challenge the will of God, but also brought into a state of entire devotement and obedience to God. The believer's will becomes one with the will of God, totally yielded to Him, pure in all its devotions to God. Believers willingly follow Christ in obedience not because they are compelled to do so but because this is their supreme and joyful desire.

2. *Entire sanctification is wrought by the baptism with the Holy Spirit.* The baptism of the Holy Spirit refines our natures of the dross of sin that remains following conversion (see Matt. 3:11-12; Mal. 3:1-3). At conversion we are indwelt by the Spirit (1 Cor. 3:16; 6:19; Rom. 8:9), but we must be "filled" with the Holy Spirit so that Christ may truly indwell

justified

us (Eph. 3:14-19; 5:17-18). We are entirely sanctified by the baptism with the Holy Spirit. This cleansing or purification makes us holy but also creates the unity of perfect love in Christ's Body, the Church, for which Christ prayed (John 17:17-26). Both purity (2 Cor. 7:1) and power (Acts 1:8) are marks of one who is entirely sanctified.

3. *Entire sanctification is provided by the blood of Jesus.* Entire sanctification is not a result of one's striving. It is an integral part of Christ's atonement (Heb. 13:12). The faith that opens the door to His provision of entire sanctification is preceded by a complete and consummate commitment of oneself to the total will of God, including everything one knows and does not know. The Holy Spirit confirms this kind of total commitment (Rom. 8:16). This assurance, which is distinctive in Wesleyan circles, rests upon God's Word and promise, the fact that all condemnation is removed, and evidence of the fruit of the Spirit in one's life (Gal. 5:22-25).

4. *Entire sanctification is known by various terms.* Terms such as "Christian perfection," "perfect love," "heart purity," "the baptism with the Holy Spirit," "the fullness of the blessing," and "Christian holiness" represent the different phases of the experience of entire sanctification.

"Perfect" or "perfection" in biblical usage means fulfilling the purpose for which a thing or person is made, not perfect in the sense of "faultless" (see 1 Thess. 3:10). Men and women were created to love God with all their souls, minds, and strength, and their neighbors as themselves. This way of living, or "Christian perfection" (1 Thess. 3:12-13), is made possible by the indwelling and enabling of the Holy Spirit.

Entire sanctification, then, is a divine work that instantaneously by faith brings freedom or cleansing from original sin, assurance through the abiding presence of the Holy Spirit, who empowers for service, and entire devotement to God.

5. *There is a distinction between a pure heart and a mature character.* We have "this treasure in earthen vessels" (2 Cor. 4:7, KJV), in frail, human bodies. A "pure heart" is obtained in an instant, the result of entire sanctification; a "ma-

justification

sanctification

ture character" is the result of growth in grace, requiring time.

We reject the notion that sin, "properly so called" (as Wesley defined it), is any deviation from the absolute law of God—any lack of conformity, any falling short. The most saintly among us on occasion fall short. The apostle Paul said, "All have sinned [past tense] and do now [present tense] come short of the glory of God" (Rom. 3:23, author's translation). This distinguishes sin from omission or error.

We can be freed from sin in its primary sense, which involves a compliance of the will, and can be granted a pure heart in an instant. However, we are not freed instantly from mistakes, ignorance, poor judgment, and so on. These are to be corrected or improved, and character is to be developed through growth in grace, which also is effected by the grace of God.

6. *Entire sanctification includes the impulse to grow in grace.* This impulse to grow in grace must be nurtured by processes such as regular worship and fellowship with other saints, study of God's Word and prayers, and exercises of compassion to the needy. When growth is stymied or does not occur at all, we are in danger of becoming ineffective witnesses to the grace of God and of losing the sanctifying and transforming power of God in our lives. Progress in Christlikeness is progress in holiness, and that is the antidote to ineffective and fruitless living.

John A. Knight is a general superintendent emeritus in the Church of the Nazarene.

Word Study

Sanctify—from the Latin *sanctus,* meaning "sacred." To sanctify is to set apart for sacred use.

Consecrate also means "to dedicate to a sacred purpose." "Sanctify" and "consecrate" come from the same Indo-European root *sak-,* "to sanctify."

As Christians, we consecrate ourselves to God, but only He can fulfill the second meaning of "sanctify"—"to make holy; to purify."

When we give ourselves wholly to God's purposes, He fills us with His Spirit, making us pure and holy in His sight.

Quote Rack

Here is God's supreme challenge to His creature, His will for us, that we should come into such actual experiential relationship with himself that we can in reality worship Him in the beauty of holiness. Here is a beauty, not of inanimate quality, not a beauty granted His creatures arbitrarily, but a beauty that man, creature of will and intelligence, can possess and which will identify him with his God, bringing glory and praise to the One who made him.

—H. V. Miller
General Superintendent, 1940-1948

Witnesses to the Faith

Joe grew up in a Catholic home with an alcoholic father who sometimes became violent. His parents divorced when he was 14, but Joe continued to serve as an altar boy until he was 18. During this time, he began following in the footsteps of his father, drinking, smoking, and using drugs. Eventually he sought counseling and gave up drugs, feeling that this step and his affiliation with the Catholic Church meant he knew Jesus.

Still, he continued to do things he knew were wrong and tried to hide them from his wife and sons. One Sunday the pastor's words burned on his heart: "Empty yourself of yourself." Joe took an empty shell and wrote inside what he felt God was saying to him: "Don't be scared. Open your shell. Give it to me." Joe prayed for forgiveness of his sins, but he knew he had not yet emptied the shell of his life entirely. Then Joe heard the calling of the Holy Spirit and prayed for God to sanctify him completely. "God knocked," Joe witnesses. "I knew right then it was time for me to give up my old life. It was time for me to follow my real Father's footsteps."

Ponder and Pursue

1. The Old Testament is filled with stories of God sanctifying (setting apart for holy use) a variety of things and people. Read how God sanctified the nation of Israel (Ezek. 37:28), a mountain (Exod. 19:23), the Sabbath (Gen. 2:3), the Tent of Meeting (Exod.

29:42-43). What did God tell the people to sanctify as holy to him in the following verses?

Exod. 29:37

Exod. 30:25

Lev. 2:10

2. Anything that was separated to be used for God's purposes only was called holy. How does this expand your understanding of personal holiness in Lev. 11:44, when God called for us to consecrate ourselves?

3. The experience of entire sanctification is known by several terms. Search these scriptures for examples:

"Christian perfection" and "perfect love": Deut. 30:6; Matt. 5:43-48; 22:37-40; Rom. 12:9-21; 13:8-10; 1 Cor. 13; Phil. 3:10-15; Heb. 6:1; 1 John 4:17-18.

"Heart purity": Matt. 5:8; Acts 15:8-9; 1 Pet. 1:22; 1 John 3:3.

"Baptism with the Holy Spirit": Jer. 31:31-34; Ezek. 36:25-27; Mal. 3:2-3; Matt. 3:11-12; Luke 3:16-17; Acts 1:5; 2:1-4; 15:8-9.

"Fullness of the blessing": Rom. 15:29.

"Christian holiness": Matt. 5:1—7:29; John 15:1-11; Rom. 12:1—15:3; 2 Cor. 7:1; Eph. 4:17—5:20; Phil. 1:9-11; 3:12-15; Col. 2:20—3:17; 1 Thess. 3:13; 4:7-8; 5:23; 2 Tim. 2:19-22; Heb. 10:19-25; 12:14; 13:20-21; 1 Pet. 1:15-16; 2 Pet. 1:1-11; 3:18; Jude 20-21.

Additional Scripture References

John 7:37-39; 14:15-23; 17:6-20; Rom. 6:11-13, 19; 8:1-4, 8-14; 2 Cor. 6:14—7:1; Gal. 2:20; 5:16-25; Eph. 3:14-21; 5:25-27; Heb. 4:9-11; 10:10-17; 12:1-2; 13:12; 1 John 1:7, 9.

11
THE CHURCH

We believe in the Church, the community that confesses Jesus Christ as Lord, the covenant people of God made new in Christ, the Body of Christ called together by the Holy Spirit through the Word.

God calls the Church to express its life in the unity and fellowship of the Spirit; in worship through the preaching of the Word, observance of the sacraments, and ministry in His name; by obedience to Christ and mutual accountability.

The mission of the Church in the world is to continue the redemptive work of Christ in the power of the Spirit through holy living, evangelism, discipleship, and service.

The Church is a historical reality, which organizes itself in culturally conditioned forms; exists both as local congregations and as a universal body; sets apart persons called of God for specific ministries. God calls the Church to live under His rule in anticipation of the consummation at the coming of our Lord Jesus Christ.

—*Manual*, Article 11

The Church belongs to God. Peter refers to the Church as "God's own people" in 1 Pet. 2:9 (NRSV), clearly expressing the intimacy with which God relates to the Church. In this verse the apostle characterizes the Church as "a chosen race, a royal priesthood, a holy nation." These definitions illustrate the utter seriousness with which the early Christians understood the Church. They also suggest that the Church is crucial to what God is doing in the world right now. The Church is one way—perhaps the most important way—that the presence of God becomes manifest to the world. The presence of God in the world is linked to the physical presence of the Church. It is the Church that in obedience sets Paul and Barnabas apart as missionaries (Acts 13:2). It is the Church that decides not to mandate circumcision as a prerequisite for Gentiles becoming part of the Church (15:8-9).

Article 11 in the *Manual of the Church of the Nazarene* underscores the importance of the Church. It begins with the simple statement that the Church is a community constituted by the confession of Jesus Christ as Lord. The central event of the New Testament is the birth, death, and resurrection of Jesus Christ. Peter confesses Jesus as Lord, and it is upon this confession that the Church is to be understood (Matt. 16:16-18). Before the Sanhedrin Peter proclaims, "There is salvation in . . . no other name under heaven" (Acts 4:12, NRSV). It is the Church that will proclaim this salvation in the name of Jesus. As the Church grapples with what to do with the Gentiles, Peter declares, "I truly understand that God shows no partiality" (Acts 10:34, NRSV). The confession of Jesus Christ as Lord lands on earth in the midst of God's own people.

The Church stands in continuity with what God has always been doing. The Church is a covenant people and as such is part of what God did in the call of Abraham and the promise to David. To a covenant people, the relationship established with Moses becomes the "law within them" (Jer. 31:33, NRSV). While God has spoken in the past by various means, He has now spoken in Jesus and established the Church as His Body. The Church is made concrete in the world by its existence as the people of God, the Body of Christ, and the temple of the Holy Spirit. By the power of the Spirit, the Word is preached, and Jesus Christ is confessed as Lord.

Article 11 affirms that the Church exists in unity and fel-

lowship by the Spirit (Gal. 3:28). This is not about style of
music or color of carpet. It is not about nationality or gender.
The Church is called to reflect the very life of God. The triune
God defines unity as communion, and in this profound mystery the unity of the Church exists. The unity is expressed
through worship by preaching, sacraments, ministry, obedience, and mutual accountability.

The mission of the Church is "to continue the redemptive
work of Christ" (*Manual*, Article 11). This happens only in the
power of the Spirit. The work of the Church becomes tangible
in holy living, evangelism, discipleship, and service. The
Church is not just an idea; it is a set of practices. And in
these practices people are invited into the very life of God so
the lost will be redeemed and the saints equipped.

The Church exists in time and space in diverse cultures. It
is a congregation of 50 in Maine, of 1,600 in Oregon, and of
the faithful in Mozambique. It has survived the rise and fall
of great civilizations. It is structured liturgy and spontaneous
praise. Some worship with organ and piano, others with
drums and guitars. The Church is men in coats and ties and
teens in jeans and T-shirts. God finds expression in the
Church in the freedom of the Spirit. We sit in a church congregation established in one place at one time, but we also
are the Church, alive across all places and all times. This
earthly reality called the Church sets people apart for ministry. While the Church plants its feet in history, it lifts its
eyes toward heaven. For the time being the Church waits, but
it does not wait passively. Rather, as we encourage one another in expectation, we are compelled to offer praise to God
and invitation to the lost. Finally, the Church is not our labor
alone; it is the mighty work of God in history.

The Church is God's own people, a physical and spiritual
reminder that God is not done yet. It is the Spirit-engen-
dered fellowship of the forgiven calling to people bound in
sin and darkness. The Church welcomes, disciplines, witnesses, remembers, encourages, bears others' burdens, and an-
ticipates the return of the One it confesses as Lord. The

Church enables God to have an address, a door, an altar, and hands and feet. It is where God helps outcasts understand that they have now become His own people.

Henry W. Spaulding II is professor of theology and philosophy at Trevecca Nazarene University in Nashville.

Word Study

Church—from the Late Greek *kūriakon*, meaning "the Lord's." It has come to mean "the Lord's house." "Church" refers not only to the location of a congregation but also, and especially, to the congregation itself. The "universal Church" (note capitalization) refers to the company of all Christians as one spiritual body.

Some early creeds, such as the Apostles' Creed, refer to the "catholic Church" (note lowercase "catholic" and capitalized "Church"). This use of "catholic" is synonymous with "universal" (all Christian believers everywhere) and is not to be confused with the Roman Catholic Church, one particular branch of Christianity.

Quote Rack

The Christian Church does not want and does not need members because of a job it has to do. The Christian Church has a secret at her heart and she wants to share it. Whenever one, by repentance and forgiveness, enters this community of grace, he discovers life's end, and he too will be constrained to let this life flow out in appropriate channels. Thrilling and costly projects will come into existence, but not as ends in themselves, and the group will not become a means to [such ends]. The group will never forget that one of its primary functions is to up build the members in love.

—William T. Ham, *Candles of the Lord*

Witnesses to the Faith

Vern and Luz Tamayo helped plant the Taytay Church of the Nazarene in a bank building near Manila, Philippines. In New Testament fashion, the church grew quickly. Even though one awful day Vern was tragically killed, their evangelistic efforts live on. On the Sunday after his death, 50 people completed four weeks of intensive discipleship and were received into church membership.

The people of the Taytay Church surrounded Luz and her three sons with love and support, eventually asking her to become their pastor. Today this church plant is a thriving ministry of marketplace evangelism, camps, campus ministries, sports evangelism, jail ministries, clinic evangelism, and motocross evangelism. On the church's 23rd anniversary, under Luz's ministry, 2,423 people attended. This church plant is now planting churches out of itself.

Ponder and Pursue

1 Cor. 12 is a metaphorical picture of the local church as a body —the Body of Christ. The emphasis is on diversity within unity.

1. What is the overarching unifying principle within the Body with such diverse parts? (See vv. 4-6, 12-13.)

2. Why have we been given such a variety of gifts, roles, personalities, and cultures? (See vv. 14-20, 28.)

3. For what reasons are we to remain in unity despite our individual diversity? (See vv. 21-27.)

4. How does 1 Cor. 12 help you better understand your church and your role within it? How can this help you deal with differences of agreement?

Additional Scripture References

Exod. 19:3; Jer. 31:33; Matt. 8:11; 10:7; 16:13-19, 24; 18:15-20; 28:19-20; John 17:14-26; 20:21-23; Acts 1:7-8; 2:32-47; 6:1-2; 13:1; 14:23; Rom. 2:28-29; 4:16; 10:9-15; 11:13-32; 12:1-8; 15:1-3; 1 Cor. 3:5-9; 7:17; 11:1, 17-33; 14:26-40; 2 Cor. 5:11—6:1; Gal. 5:6, 13-14; 6:1-5, 15; Eph. 4:1-17; 5:25-27; Phil. 2:1-16; 1 Thess. 4:1-12; 1 Tim. 4:13; Heb. 10:19-25; 1 Pet. 1:1-2, 13; 2:4-12, 21; 4:1-2, 10-11; 1 John 4:17; Jude 24; Rev. 5:9-10.

12
BAPTISM

We believe that Christian baptism, commanded by our Lord, is a sacrament signifying acceptance of the benefits of the atonement of Jesus Christ, to be administered to believers and declarative of their faith in Jesus Christ as their Savior, and full purpose of obedience in holiness and righteousness.

Baptism being a symbol of the new covenant, young children may be baptized, upon request of parents or guardians who shall give assurance for them of necessary Christian training.

Baptism may be administered by sprinkling, pouring, or immersion, according to the choice of the applicant.

—*Manual*, Article 12

In India a Nazarene pastor pours water on the heads of a couple kneeling before him in a stony brook. In Peru a Nazarene missionary standing in a reservoir immerses baptismal candidates one by one. And at a district assembly in Texas, seven infants are presented by their parents to General Superintendent H. F. Reynolds, who baptizes each by sprinkling. All are recognized by the Church of the Nazarene as valid Christian baptisms.

Ours is a "means of grace" tradition. With the Protestant reformers, Wesleyans understand faith as God's ordained vehicle through which we appropriate divine grace. But God communicates that grace to our faith "receptors" through various means: the preached gospel, the sacraments, Bible study, prayer, meditation, fasting, and Christian fellowship, among others.

Baptism and the Lord's Supper, recognized universally as sacraments of the Church, reenact essential facets of the gospel. Both require our participation.

Sacraments engage the believer but always do so within the context of the Church, the community whose worship centers in Christ. Often Christians experience strong personal emotions while participating in sacramental acts, but the primary purpose of sacraments is to shape the Body of Christ. Sacraments give the Church coherence and continuity across space and time.

Both baptism and the Lord's Supper are based on "dominical injunctions"; that is, they are acts of worship Jesus our Lord *(domine)* instructed His followers to observe. But Jesus did more than instruct—He set the example. We take sacraments seriously because true disciples heed their Master's instructions and conform to His pattern.

Baptism is the sacrament of initiation into the Church. Though performed by ordained ministers of one denomination or another, baptism is not sectarian. It signifies initiation into the Church Universal, uniting us with a larger fellowship of believers, though we experience that wider fellowship locally.

Baptism functions as a means of grace in several ways. First, the baptized person publicly receives the Church and its gifts, including aids to spiritual growth, discipline, and accountability. The Church in turn receives the baptized person's gifts and graces and integrates them into its corporate witness. At the most elemental level, baptism calls us to public ministry. As part of the Body of Christ, we daily go into the world to minister through our vocations and lives as representatives of Christ and His Church.

The two types of baptism, infant baptism and believer's baptism, have ancient roots in the Christian Church, and the

Church of the Nazarene permits both. Parents may present infant children for baptism or choose not to do so. Some Nazarene founders came from churches that practiced one type, others from backgrounds that preferred the other. The three parent bodies that merged to create the Church of the Nazarene each allowed liberty of conscience on this issue. That has been the Nazarene way ever since.

Infant baptism has been more widely practiced throughout Christian history. In Eastern Orthodoxy, Catholicism, and in most Protestant churches, a basic logic for infant baptism has been consistently maintained. It has been viewed as a Christian analogy to the Jewish rite of circumcision, marking initiation into a covenant community.[1] Wesleyans have an additional rationale. We view God's grace in Christ as universal, extended as an offer to all. On this basis, we teach that infants are covered by the benefits of Christ's atonement until they reach the age of moral accountability. Among us, infant baptism does not impart saving grace but signifies a grace already present. It is as truly an outward sign of inward grace as baptism is for adults whose act acknowledges their sins forgiven.

Believers' baptism, a minority position through much of Christian history, has grown increasingly popular over the past two centuries.[2] During the 20th century, its popularity has increased among Nazarenes and is the most common type of baptism we practice today. Adult, or believer's, bap-

---

1. Some of the Protestant churches in which infant baptism predominates are all Lutheran, Anglican, Congregationalist, Presbyterian, and Reformed churches and most Methodist denominations.

2. Churches that strictly affirm believer's baptism include Mennonites, Church of the Brethren, Disciples and Churches of Christ, all Baptists, and most Pentecostal denominations. In North America the growth of believer's baptism is due largely to the 20th-century surge of Baptists and Pentecostals. In global Christianity, it is due largely to Pentecostalism's popularity.

tism is a public declaration that the believer has repented of his or her sins, received Christ's forgiveness, and seeks to amend his or her life under the Holy Spirit's supervision. It also signifies the believer's conscious and informed decision to unite with the Church.

Christian baptism has been administered in three modes: sprinkling, pouring, and immersion. Nazarenes do not insist on a certain mode. We permit candidates (or parents, in the case of infants) to exercise a conscientious choice.

J. B. Chapman, one of our wisest leaders, stated that neither the time in life nor the mode of baptism is as important as its fact. And, he insisted, "It is expected that people who unite with the Church of the Nazarene shall have some water by some mode" (*Herald of Holiness*, Dec. 13, 1922).

Stan Ingersol is manager of Nazarene Archives at the international headquarters of the Church of the Nazarene in Kansas City.

Word Study

Sacrament—from the Latin *sacrre*, meaning "to consecrate." A sacrament is a Christian rite that symbolizes divine grace. Visible outward elements that are blessed or consecrated, such as water, symbolize invisible inner workings of God's grace. John Wesley defined sacrament as "an outward sign of inward grace, and a means whereby we receive the same" (*Works*, 5:188). The sacraments varied in number for a thousand years in Early Church history. In the 12th century, seven were defended, which the Catholic Church and Eastern Orthodoxy still observe. During the 16th century, Protestant reformers rejected five of these. Today most Protestant churches, including the Church of the Nazarene, observe two: baptism and the Lord's Supper.

Quote Rack

No sacramental act achieves anything unless it is an outward symbol of what really happens inwardly in experience. The test of that is the reality of the new life as exhibited in its ethical consequences. "How can we who are dead to sin live any longer in sin?" If baptism is a real dying and rising again, then it is indeed a profound revolution in the personal life, a revolution which is simply bound to show itself in a new moral character.

—C. Harold Dodd, *The Meaning of Paul for Today*

In *For Whom the Bell Tolls*, John Donne wrote, "The church is . . . universal, so are all her actions; all that she does belongs to all. When she baptizes a child, that action concerns me; for that child is thereby connected to that body which is my head too, and ingrafted into that body whereof I am a member." Far beyond casual observers of the ceremony of baptism, each member of the Body of Christ is charged with the responsibility of leading, nurturing, protecting, and caring for the new Christian, just as a family would a new infant.

Footprints

While the history of the Church of the Nazarene records the baptismal preferences of early leaders, the church soon settled on emphasizing significance over methods. Although J. B. Chapman, early editor of *Herald of Holiness* and general superintendent, was an immersionist, he defended other methods and counseled ministers to baptize by modes other than their personal preferences rather than make new believers wait for a minister in wholehearted agreement with their mode of choice (*Herald of Holiness*, December 13, 1922).

Mary Lee Cagle, a key early Nazarene preacher, first defended pouring as the only scriptural mode of baptism. But after 1904, she came to embrace the ideal of allowing each baptismal candidate to choose the mode of baptism. In a service in New Mexico, she and her husband baptized believers in "every way under the sun—by every mode possible. They dipped—they plunged—they sprinkled and they baptized babies. It was a time of rejoicing; and the shouts of the redeemed echoed and re-echoed through the hills" (*Life and Work of Mary Lee Cagle*).

Early general superintendents Phineas F. Bresee, Hiram F. Reynolds, Roy T. Williams, J. B. Chapman, and John W. Goodwin were often sought out at district assemblies to baptize infants. Entries in district assembly proceedings illustrate the one-time popularity of this practice: "At 2 o'clock Dr. Reynolds baptized six babies, which occasion was a blessing to all. After this a great ordination service followed" (*Journal*, Eastern Oklahoma District, 1924).

Scripture References

Matt. 3:1-7; 28:16-20; Acts 2:37-41; 8:35-39; 10:44-48; 16:29-34; 19:1-6; Rom. 6:3-4; Gal. 3:26-28; Col. 2:12; 1 Pet. 3:18-22.

13

THE LORD'S SUPPER

We believe that the Memorial and Communion Supper instituted by our Lord and Savior Jesus Christ is essentially a New Testament sacrament, declarative of His sacrificial death, through the merits of which believers have life and salvation and promise of all spiritual blessings in Christ. It is distinctively for those who are prepared for reverent appreciation of its significance, and by it they show forth the Lord's death till He come again. It being the Communion feast, only those who have faith in Christ and love for the saints should be called to participate therein.

—*Manual*, Article 13

Can you imagine being with the 12 disciples as they walked with Jesus in Galilee and Judea? In our Christian walk today, is it possible to be in the presence of Jesus in a manner that closely duplicates the experience of the disciples? We pray, read the Bible, worship, and minister to others, but our experience is not quite the same as theirs.

The disciples were in the physical presence of Jesus. They could reach out and touch His real, flesh-and-blood body. The good news is that He has provided a way for us to do virtually the same thing when we reach out and take the bread that He said is His body and drink the cup that He said is His blood. The 12 disciples had no great advantage over us. At the Communion table we, too, are in Christ's presence, very much as they were. Good news indeed.

The sacrament of the Lord's Supper is known by various names in the New Testament and in Christian history: Communion, Holy Communion, the Supper, the Breaking of Bread, the Table of the Lord, and Eucharist.

At Christ's table we affirm at least five truths.

1. *The Supper is a commemoration in accordance with Christ's words: "Do this in remembrance of me" (Luke 22:19).* In the Old Testament, God's people were admonished to not forget the God who had delivered them from Egypt. Likewise, we are to remember Christ's atoning work in bringing us out of sin's bondage. It is thus a memorial, but it is much more.

2. *The Supper is a celebration in which we give thanks for our redemption.* The word "Eucharist" comes from a Greek verb meaning "to be thankful." A form of the word is used in each of the four New Testament accounts of the Last Supper (Matt. 26:26-30; Mark 14:22-26; Luke 22:14-20; and 1 Cor. 11:23-26) when Jesus gave thanks over the bread before giving it to the disciples. Eucharist is a time of thanksgiving, like the ancient harvest festivals.

Just as Jews celebrated God's mighty redemptive acts by eating and drinking at various Old Covenant festivals, so Christians celebrate the work of God in His acts of redemption through Jesus Christ by eating and drinking at the Eucharist. To her detriment, the Church has sometimes forgotten the influence of Jewish worship on Christian Eucharistic thought and practice, allowing Christian worship to lose its robustness and become weak and sentimental.

In the Early Church the Eucharist was an occasion of joyful celebration. It was a festive occasion, not a solemn, mournful one. As the centuries passed, the more mournful note became predominant and has persisted far too long in many churches. We need to recover the "mealness" of this meal. It represents fiesta, not funeral. Like mealtimes in happy families, the Lord's Supper should be a joyful time when God's family gathers. Of course, the solemn note should not be entirely missing as we consider the awful cost God paid at Calvary for our redemption. But we should quickly turn from Calvary to Easter, from Crucifixion to Resurrection and to the risen Christ's presence with us at the Table, just as He was present with the two disciples at Emmaus (Luke 24:30-32).

3. *The Supper is a presentation in which we offer ourselves as living sacrifices (Rom. 12:1).* Sacrifice was important in the religion of Israel. It is pervasive in the Book of Hebrews and figures prominently in the language Jesus used at the institution of the Supper (see Matt. 26:28). The invitation to Christ's table is a call "to be a holy priesthood, offering spiritual sacrifices acceptable to God through Jesus Christ" (1 Pet. 2:5).

4. *The Eucharist is a participation in the blood and body of Christ (1 Cor. 10:16).* The Greek word *koinonia* in that verse may be translated as "fellowship," "sharing," or "participation." But Paul cautions against "unworthy" participation (1 Cor. 11:27). Unfortunately, a misunderstanding of Paul's warning has kept away from the Table some sensitive souls who felt unworthy. Actually, nobody is ever really worthy to be invited to Christ's table. If worthiness were the requirement, nobody could ever come to the Supper. But the context shows that to eat unworthily is to eat "without recognizing the body" (v. 29) by selfishly refusing to share and denying fellowship, thereby violating *koinonia*.

5. *The Supper means anticipation as we look toward the end of the age.* It is a foretaste, an appetizer for the final feast in the kingdom of God. It is a real taste but not the full taste. The full taste awaits that day "when the times will have reached their fulfillment—to bring all things in heaven and on earth together under one head, even Christ" (Eph. 1:10). Feasting at Christ's table now, we rejoice in that blessed hope.

Rob L. Staples is emeritus professor of theology at Nazarene Theological Seminary in Kansas City.

Word Study

Communion—from the Greek *koinonia*, meaning "fellowship." In 1 Cor. 10:16 (KJV) Paul relates the cup and bread to communion. Communion signifies a common bond, a genuine sharing of fellowship with our risen Lord, especially in partaking of the Lord's Supper. As George Macdonald said, "Hunger may drive the runaway child home, and he may or may not be fed at home; but he needs his mother more than his dinner. Communion with God is the one need of the soul beyond all other need" (*The Word of Jesus on Prayer*).

Q&A

1. *What is the difference in the various terms used for the Lord's Supper?*

Each highlights a significant aspect of this sacrament. "The Lord's Supper" (1 Cor. 11:20) and "the Lord's Table" (1 Cor. 10:21) both emphasize the Lord's ownership. "Communion" (1 Cor. 10:16, KJV) illustrates the fellowship or "joining in common" between God and humans made possible by the sacrifice of Christ. Church fathers began to call the occasion the "Eucharist," meaning "thanksgiving," from the blessing pronounced over the sacrament after approximately A.D. 100.

2. *Who is qualified to administer the Lord's Supper?*

Ordained elders and deacons and licensed ministers meeting requirements as set forth in the *Manual of the Church of the Nazarene* are authorized to administer the sacraments of both baptism and the Lord's Supper.

3. *Who may participate in the Lord's Supper?*

Some churches practice "closed" communion, allowing participation only by members, and others offer "open" communion to anyone. In the Church of the Nazarene, all those who have "with true repentance forsaken their sins, and have believed in Christ unto salvation" (*Manual*, par. 802) are invited to partake, regardless of church affiliation.

4. *What do we believe about the elements?*

Unlike some congregations who believe the drink and bread are spiritually, supernaturally, or substantially transformed into the body and blood of Christ, we believe the elements are symbolic of

His body and blood and that in partaking we participate in His sacrificial death.

5. *How may the elements of the Lord's Supper be presented?*

The Church of the Nazarene uses unfermented grape juice and unleavened bread or wafers. The cup may be individual or common, and distribution may be from a central or multiple locations or passed for eating and drinking in unison as a congregation.

6. *How often should the Lord's Supper be observed?*

The Bible says nothing about frequency. Until the 16th century, the Church generally celebrated the Lord's Supper weekly. Since the Reformation, there has not been a universal pattern of frequency among Protestant churches.

Footprints

The oldest congregation in the Church of the Nazarene was organized in 1887 as The People's Evangelical Church in Providence, Rhode Island. Prior to the union of Holiness churches that became the Church of the Nazarene, it operated by its own congregational manual, which included an article of faith on the Lord's Supper. Participation was so highly valued that "unnecessary absence" from communion was considered grounds for church discipline and dismissal ("Standing Rules").

Ponder and Pursue

1. As the Passover was a symbol of the old covenant (Exod. 12:1-14), the Lord's Supper is a symbol of the new covenant, sealed by Christ's death and resurrection (Matt. 26:26-29). What did the Israelites celebrate and commemorate in the Passover? How is that similar to what we celebrate and commemorate in the Lord's Supper? How are they different?

2. The church at Corinth suffered division because of the way it observed the Lord's Supper (1 Cor. 11:17-34). In what ways did the Corinthians displease God? What were Paul's instructions to them?

Additional Scripture References

Mark 14:22-25; Luke 22:17-20; John 6:28-58; 1 Cor. 10:14-21.

14
DIVINE HEALING

We believe in the Bible doctrine of divine healing and urge our people to seek to offer the prayer of faith for the healing of the sick. We also believe God heals through the means of medical science.

—*Manual*, Article 14

Consisting of two simple sentences, the article of faith on divine healing is the shortest article in the *Manual*. At first glance these few words hardly seem to touch on the same weighty matters of faith dealt with in other articles, such as sin, salvation, and the incarnation of Jesus Christ. But the affirmation the church makes in this article of faith is nevertheless important and does touch on central concerns of our faith.

First, by urging people to pray for the sick, we affirm that God cares about our physical bodies. Now and again throughout Christian history, believers have fallen into the trap of thinking that bodies are evil. Early heretics called Gnostics taught that the goal of life is to allow the "true self," the "soul," to escape the corruption of this evil physical reality. However, genuine Christian faith will not allow us to call evil what God created as good. Furthermore, we believe that what God created, God cares about. So when we exhort our people to pray for those who are ailing, we do so believing that God is concerned about the things that cause us pain and disrupt our lives in this world.

Second, in urging people to pray for the sick and in recognizing that God often works through human beings trained in medical science, we affirm our belief in a God who acts. In the scientifically driven Western society, many people are not comfortable with the idea that God "messes about" in the natural world or the world of human affairs. We much prefer explaining everything neatly and simply in terms of physical causes and effects without having to say all the time, "God did it." That may be an easier way to view the world, but it does not agree with the picture of God painted in the Bible.

The God of the Bible is a God who acts, who is engaged in the world of natural and human affairs, a God who can make things happen. We affirm that God is free to be "miraculous" when He so chooses, and we also affirm the validity of what some would call "unmiraculous" medical science. But while not all of God's works need to be categorized as miracles, that doesn't change the fact that He is behind medical healing. He bestows gifts to doctors and nurses, created a world in which certain chemicals have positive biological effects, and designed the human body in such a way that it can be largely, though apparently not completely, understood.

Of course, this does not mean that God heals every time we ask, either divinely or through medical science. Our article of faith is written as an exhortation to prayer, not as a guarantee that God will always do what we want. There is no sense in praying if we don't think God cares enough to act, but our prayers are not magical incantations that force Him to do so. God is in the business of growing the Kingdom, and sometimes His kingdom is best served in our weakness and infirmity (2 Cor. 12:7-10). These are the times when we find ourselves praying with Jesus in Gethsemane, "Yet not what I want but what you want" (Matt. 26:39, NRSV).

We believe that this physical world is not the ultimate one. Indeed, the condition of the soul is paramount. We recognize that the ultimate healing God wants to accomplish cannot be limited to the healing of mortal bodies and minds in this fallen world. We know from the Cross that God's ultimate healing is sometimes accomplished in the midst of pain and suffering. Nevertheless, we still affirm that sickness and disease do not represent life as it was created to be, and we believe that God will often, though not always, demonstrate His love and concern by acting in ways that heal and restore our physical bodies.

Whatever problems we face in determining exactly where and how God works, we still affirm as a church that He does in fact work to bring "the healing of the nations" (Rev. 22:2).

And that's why we include this article in our *Manual*. We believe in a God who acts because He cares, and that ought to lead us to care and act as well.

Timothy J. Crutcher is assistant professor of history and theology at Southern Nazarene University in Bethany, Oklahoma.

Word Study

Heal—from the Indo-European root *kailo-* through the Old English *hAl*, meaning "whole." Likewise, the word "whole" is derived from the Old Norse *heill*, meaning "healthy." To be healthy is to be whole; to be whole is to be healthy. God created our entire beings, bodies, minds, and spirits and is capable of bringing wholeness and health to every aspect of our lives. Apart from Him, we are neither whole nor healed. (See the Word Study for "holy" in chapter 3: "The Holy Spirit.")

Quote Rack

> Heal us, Emmanuel! here we are,
> Waiting to feel Thy touch:
> Deep-wounded souls to Thee repair,
> And, Saviour, we are such.
> —William Cowper, "Olney Hymns"

Witnesses to the Faith

In 1936 Orpha Speicher, a medical doctor, arrived in India as a missionary of the Church of the Nazarene. Two years earlier, another mission organization had ceded to the Nazarenes a piece of property in Washim, India. Dr. Speicher took responsibility for remodeling a former school building there into a hospital, which opened in 1938. At first Dr. Speicher had the help of only one trained nurse. As the medical staff gained the confidence of the population, a need arose to expand the hospital. Dr. Speicher took on the roles of architect and construction supervisor. The process of constructing a modern hospital continued over 15 years, and in 1946 missionary Jean Darling established the first nurses' training course. Today the India Nazarene Nurses Training College and Reynolds Memorial Hospital are operated fully by Indian Christians as a powerful witness of God's love and healing power to thousands of villagers.

Footprints

Phineas F. Bresee, the church's first general superintendent, lived in Methodist parsonages until 1894, when he and his wife moved into the home of their doctor son, Paul Bresee, in Los Angeles, where they resided until their deaths. In keeping with the practice of the time, Paul Bresee's office was in the home itself, and patients came and went all day long. Paul was also his parents' physician. Paul was an active Nazarene layperson, and his wife, Ada, was one of the founders of the Nazarene missionary society and the longtime district secretary of the Southern California District.

Ponder and Pursue

1. *JEHOVAH-ROPHE*, one of the many names for God in the Bible, is translated "The Lord Who Heals." *JEHOVAH-ROPHE* implies spiritual, emotional, and physical healing. To read about "The Lord Who Heals," see Exod. 15:22-26 and Jer. 30:17. What kind of healing is implied in these verses?

2. We generally associate healing with Jesus' ministry in the New Testament. "The Lord Who Heals" was also active in the Old Testament. For examples of both, see these scriptures:

Old Testament: Gen. 2:20-22; Num. 21:4-9; 1 Sam. 1:19; 2:21; 5:10—6:12; 2 Kings 5:1-14.

New Testament: Matt. 4:23-24; 8:14-15; 12:9-13; 20:29-34; Mark 5:25-34; Luke 7:1-10, 22; 17:11-19; 22:47-51.

The apostles were also charged with the ministry of healing. See Acts 3:1-10; 5:12-16; 9:10-19; 14:8-15.

3. Many Christians have difficulty grappling with why some people are healed and some are not. For examples of how suffering can be for purposes that we in our humanity do not understand, read Ps. 73:1-5, 23-26 and Job 2:7-10. The answer lies in the sover-

eignty of God (Job 38—42:6) and in the confidence of eternal glory (2 Cor. 4:16-18).

Additional Scripture References

Ps. 103:1-5; Matt. 9:18-35; John 4:46-54; Acts 9:32-42; 1 Cor. 12:4-11; 2 Cor. 12:7-10; James 5:13-16.

15
SECOND COMING OF CHRIST

We believe that the Lord Jesus Christ will come again; that we who are alive at His coming shall not precede them that are asleep in Christ Jesus; but that, if we are abiding in Him, we shall be caught up with the risen saints to meet the Lord in the air, so that we shall ever be with the Lord.

—*Manual*, Article 15

General Douglas MacArthur stood at the water's edge and bid farewell to the soldiers stationed in the Philippines during World War II. He left them with a promise: "I shall return." Jesus stood with His disciples on the Mount of Olives and made a similar promise just before He left for heaven's home.

Most Christian articles of faith make some declaration regarding the second coming of Christ. Our reason for believing so strongly in Christ's return finds strength in the 318 New Testament references to it. Jesus himself spoke often of His return, primarily in Matt. 24—25, Mark 13, and Luke 21. Paul added a later perspective in Phil. 3 and 1 Thess. 4. Immediately following Jesus' departure, two angels comforted His disciples, saying, "This same Jesus, who has been taken from you into heaven, will come back in the same way you have seen him go into heaven" (Acts 1:11).

While not all our questions can be answered now, the Bible indicates several important things about Christ's return.

1. *What can we expect?* According to the Bible, Christ's return will include these events:

The Heavenly Father, having kept a watchful eye on the world situation throughout time, will determine when the appropriate time has arrived.

He will signal Jesus, His Son, to return bodily to earth accompanied by a mighty host of heavenly angels.

Jesus will appear in the eastern sky, visible to believers and nonbelievers alike.

His return will mark the end of time as we know it.

Resurrection, judgment, and eternal reward or punishment will await everyone who has ever lived on the earth.

2. *How can we expect it?* Around these basic facts revolves a whole series of events such as the Tribulation, the Antichrist's reign, a period of peace and prosperity, and a world-involved battle known as Armageddon. The problem with discussing these events and other end-time happenings relates to their timing and sequence. Various charts noting these events in great detail have circulated among Christians for many years. They often differ from one another significantly. This difference of opinion stems from the fact that while the Bible gives us many snapshots of things to come, it does not sequence them for us. Let me illustrate. After a family vacation, my wife, Sue, often hands me a stack of vacation photographs and says, "Organize these in sequential order for our photo album." Because I participated in the events captured on film, the task is simple. However, my friend Gary would have a harder time organizing the shots because he wasn't with us.

So the truth is that we don't know how or in what order all of these end-time events will transpire. The only thing we can say with certainty is that they will occur just as the Bible indicates.

3. *When can we expect it?* A few years ago, a good friend was so convinced of Christ's immediate return that he watched the world news daily with bated breath, ready to announce his final prediction just moments before the actual

event occurred. He preached on Christ's return every week. He's since gone on to be with the Lord, and we're still here on earth waiting. So the *when* question still goes unanswered.

I took a class on this subject during my doctoral studies. Starting with the time of the Early Church and continuing through the present, we studied each generation of Christians who believed Christ would return in its day. Which generations did we study? Every generation from the first century until now. That's right! Every group of believers throughout Church history has believed Christ's return might be immediate.

4. *How then should we live?* When Jesus' disciples pressed Him for a timeline, He answered, "It is not for you to know the times or dates the Father has set by his own authority" (Acts 1:7). Some interpret this to mean that we can't construct a timeline unless we work hard at it. I disagree. Jesus is urging us not to get caught up in end-time predictions. Rather, He admonishes us to live our Christian lives as salt and light in our world with the hope of His return drawing us ever onward.

"Keep watch," Jesus said, "because you do not know on what day your Lord will come" (Matt. 24:42). We respond with John, "Amen. Come, Lord Jesus" (Rev. 22:20).

Frank Moore is vice president for academic affairs and dean at MidAmerica Nazarene University in Olathe, Kansas.

Word Study

Parousia—from the Indo-European root *es-*, "to be," through the Greek *parousia*, "presence" or "arrival." In the ancient world, "parousia" indicated the visit of a king to one of his provinces. The Greek *parousia* entered the English language unchanged in form except for capitalization. Today in English, "Parousia" has only one meaning: the Second Coming.

An End-Times Glossary

Eschatology—the study of "last things" or the end times.

Apocalyptic—referring to the belief that the end of the world as we know it is approaching.

Tribulation—a period of upheaval during which Satan will exert control over the earth through the Antichrist.

Armageddon—the geographic location given in Revelation for the climactic battle of the end of time.

Millennial—referring to the thousand-year reign of Christ on earth *in heaven* after end-times events have brought an end to this world.

Doomsday cults—those who withdraw from the world because of its evil to wait for the end of the world, sometimes causing events to bring about their own end-times predictions.

Quote Rack

If our hopes, whatever we protest, really lie in this world instead of in the eternal order, we shall find it difficult to accept the New Testament teaching of the Second Coming. In our eyes, the job is not yet done; and such an action would be, though we would not put it so, an interference. But suppose our hope rests in the purpose of God: then we safely leave the timing of the earthly experiment to Him. Meanwhile, we do what we were told to do—to be alert and to work and pray for the spread of His Kingdom.

—J. B. Phillips, *New Testament Christianity*

We are living "between the times"—the time of Christ's resurrection and the new age of the Spirit, and the time of fulfillment in Christ. Life in the Spirit is a pledge, a "down-payment," on the final kingdom of shalom. In the meantime, we are to be signs of the kingdom which is, and which is coming.   —David Kirk

The Second Coming is not the return of a Lord who has been absent, but the complete and victorious breaking through of a presence that has been hitherto partially hidden by the veil of sin and evil. The resurrected mode of Christ's existence will in this event be so thoroughly actualized in the world that it can no longer be hidden.   —Rob L. Staples, *Words of Faith*

Ponder and Pursue

The Second Coming is mentioned 318 times in the New Testament. While there are end-times events and times that we cannot predict and in fact are not meant to know, the Word of God gives definite prophecies about Christ's Second Coming that we can know for sure. Examine the following scriptures.

Christ will come to earth a second time. Matt. 24:27, 30; Luke 21:27; Acts 1:11; Rev. 1:7-8.

The exact time of His return is unknown. Matt. 24:36, 44; 25:13; 1 Thess. 5:2; Rev. 16:15.

Definite signs will point to His return. Matt. 24:1-35; 2 Thess. 2:3-4; 1 Tim. 4:1; 2 Tim. 3:1-5.

Additional Scripture References

Matt. 25:31-46; John 14:1-3; Acts 1:9-11; Phil. 3:20-21; 1 Thess. 4:13-18; Titus 2:11-14; Heb. 9:26-28; 2 Pet. 3:3-15; Rev. 22:7-20.

16

RESURRECTION, JUDGMENT, AND DESTINY

We believe in the resurrection of the dead, that the bodies both of the just and of the unjust shall be raised to life and united with their spirits—"they that have done good, unto the resurrection of life; and they that have done evil, unto the resurrection of damnation."

We believe in future judgment in which every person shall appear before God to be judged according to his or her deeds in this life.

We believe that glorious and everlasting life is assured to all who savingly believe in, and obediently follow, Jesus Christ our Lord; and that the finally impenitent shall suffer eternally in hell.

—*Manual*, Article 16

The concluding article of faith concerns, appropriately, the end of human life. At first glance it might appear foreboding in its anticipation of judgment. But in fact this article in all its parts is an affirmation of God's gracious plan for humanity.

A rightful understanding of judgment is as surely about a

gracious gift as it is about the anticipation of heaven. God has given humanity the weighty gift of significance. Our decisions matter. Our choices are real. How we live makes a difference. A quick response might suggest that we would be better off without the responsibility for this fearsome gift. Wouldn't it be better if the story came out the same no matter what we do?

Some years ago a movie explored that possibility by playing out the plight of a person captured in a reality in which his choices and actions had no effect. Each new day started over the same regardless of what he did. Good choices, bad choices, self-destruction, noble sacrifice—all disappeared as if they had never happened. What might seem an attractive option quickly revealed its underlying futility. The leading character found that his life had no meaning, no significance. His release to live in a way that had consequences made real life possible.

God has given us that gift. We matter. What we do matters. It is a weighty gift, full of profound and sometimes frightening possibilities. But it *is* a gift.

It is important also to recognize the character and spirit of judgment. A strong affirmation of consequences does not mean God enjoys or takes satisfaction in His final judgment of disobedience. Believing that God has some kind of "now you're going to get what you deserve" spirit of satisfaction is a projection of our human inclination to vindication. To the contrary, God's spirit can be observed in Jesus when He wept over the doomed city of Jerusalem. "O Jerusalem, Jerusalem, you who kill the prophets and stone those sent to you, how often I have longed to gather your children together, as a hen gathers her chicks under her wings, but you were not willing" (Matt. 23:37). God will finally judge, but it will be a day of divine sadness for those who have rejected Him.

C. S. Lewis offers a helpful description of Judgment Day in his book *The Great Divorce*. On that day, he suggests, only two kinds of people will stand before God: those who have said to God, "Thy will be done," and surrendered to the life-giving lordship of Christ; and those to whom God will finally, reluctantly, say, "Thy will be done." The latter will be released to their own lordship. The judgment they suffer will, in fact, be their own. The God who has given us the significance of human freedom must at last recognize our insistent declaration of independence.

The end of the story is all about gifts. Having given us significance and, therefore, consequences, God offers the hope of eternal life, which transcends all the merit of any of our actions. We are offered an outcome beyond our farthest reach.

The life offered to us is everlasting. The biblical meaning of this kind of life tells us as much about the quality of life as how long it lasts. It is life at its fullest. It is life at its most vital and rich. It has wholeness and depth. It is the kind of life that not only lasts forever but also lasts forever fully and completely in God's presence. It is life unspeakably more abundant than we can presently imagine. Death in all its forms—brokenness, sorrow, sickness, loneliness, alienation—will be overcome with healing and wholeness. "When the perishable has been clothed with the imperishable, and the mortal with immortality, then the saying that is written will come true: 'Death has been swallowed up in victory'" (1 Cor. 15:54).

Like the rest of God's story for us, the end of the story is good news. God honors us, blessing us with real potential and indescribable hope. His vision for us goes beyond this brief, mortal life. He calls us to an understanding of ourselves and our lives that lifts us to a higher place of enduring hope. This hope not only points to an anticipated future but also helps us understand and live our lives right now. Because this is the future God has for us, we can—and must—live faithfully and confidently for Him right where we are. We already know how the story ends.

Carl M. Leth is professor of theology and chair of the Division of Religion and Philosophy at Olivet Nazarene University in Kankakee, Illinois.

Word Study

Destiny—from the Indo-European root *stā-*, meaning "to stand," through the Latin *dēstināre*, "to make firm, establish." One's destiny is "the inevitable or necessary fate to which a particular person or thing is destined." However, unlike the understanding of fate as an outcome predestined by an unknown force or uncontrollable events, the Word of God teaches that our eternal destiny is determined by God's righteous judgment of our free choices and deeds in life. Eternal life is open to all who choose to "savingly believe in, and obediently follow, Jesus Christ our Lord" (*Manual*, Article 16).

Quote Rack

Now since our eternal state is as certainly ours, as our present state; since we are as certainly to live forever, as we now live at all; it is plain, that we cannot judge of the value of any particular time, as to us, but by comparing it to that eternal duration, for which we are created. . . .

Till the end of time, God is compassionate and long-suffering, and continues to every creature a power of choosing life or death, water or fire; but when the end of time is come, there is an end of choice, and the last judgment is only a putting everyone into the full and sole possession of that which he has chosen.

—William Law, *An Appeal to All That Doubt*

Ponder and Pursue

1. What will happen to those who have died before the Second Coming? John 5:25-29; 11:21-27; 1 Cor. 15:12-58; 1 Thess. 4:13-18; Rev. 20:11-13.

2. Who has the Father chosen to serve as judge? John 5:22-23, 26-27; 2 Tim. 4:1.

3. Who will be judged? Matt. 25:31-32; 2 Cor. 5:10.

4. What is the final destiny as a result of judgment? Matt. 25:31-46; Rom. 2:5-11; Rev. 20:15.

Additional Scripture References

Gen. 18:25; 1 Sam. 2:10; Ps. 50:6; Isa. 26:19; Dan. 12:2-3; Mark 9:43-48; Luke 16:19-31; 20:27-38; John 3:16-18; Acts 17:30-31; Rom. 2:1-16; 14:7-12; 2 Thess. 1:5-10; Rev. 22:1-15.